**INTO THE
HEART OF
THE MIND**

INTO THE HEART OF THE MIND

An American Quest for Artificial Intelligence

FRANK ROSE

1817

HARPER & ROW, PUBLISHERS, New York
Cambridge, Philadelphia, San Francisco, London
Mexico City, São Paulo, Singapore, Sydney

Portions of this work originally appeared in somewhat different form in *Esquire*.

INTO THE HEART OF THE MIND. Copyright © 1984 by Frank Rose. All rights reserved. Printed in the United States of America. No part of this book may be used or reproduced in any manner whatsoever without written permission except in the case of brief quotations embodied in critical articles and reviews. For information address Harper & Row, Publishers, Inc., 10 East 53rd Street, New York, N.Y. 10022. Published simultaneously in Canada by Fitzhenry & Whiteside Limited, Toronto.

FIRST EDITION

Designer: Helene Berinsky

Library of Congress Cataloging in Publication Data

Rose, Frank.

　Into the heart of the mind.

　　1. Artificial intelligence. 2. Computers.
3. Machine learning. I. Title.
Q335.R65　1984　　001.53′5　　83-48380
ISBN 0-06-015306-7

84 85 86 87 88 10 9 8 7 6 5 4 3 2 1

For Beth

Contents

Acknowledgments

This book had its genesis in a series of articles for *Esquire*, each of which was edited and guided into print by Marilyn Johnson. To Marilyn, who was a source of endless inspiration and enthusiasm; to my subsequent editor, Gene Stone; and of course to Phillip Moffitt, who supported me throughout, I owe a great deal of gratitude.

A number of people helped make the writing of this book easier. Among them are Randy Shilts, Dan Yoder, and Janie Krohn, who made life possible during the months of research; Ron Lichty, whose generosity contributed greatly to the result; and Kathy Ku, George Moore, and Lanny Fields, who lent me their expertise at critical moments. I'm particularly indebted to the subjects of this book and to a number of their colleagues in the computer science division at Berkeley for their patience in explaining to me the mysteries of computation.

Finally, I owe a special debt of gratitude to my agent, Mary Evans, and to my editor, Craig Nelson, whose faith and intuition led directly to the book in hand. And I'd like to thank the staff at Harper & Row, especially Coral Tysliava, whose keen eyes proved conclusively that human beings are still superior to computers.

INTO THE
HEART OF
THE MIND

Prologue

Young Frankenstein was the Computer Club's second movie. The first movie they'd tried to show had been a disaster: It wasn't advertised until three days ahead of time, and it was screened in a classroom on Halloween night, and only about a dozen people showed up. This time the Events Committee had been a little more careful. They'd rented the auditorium of Wheeler Hall, a giant marble wedding-cake building in the middle of campus. They'd had posters on every available bulletin board for weeks. And although they didn't have too many films to choose from— *2001* wasn't available, for instance—the picture they'd come up with was sure to draw a crowd. At Berkeley, California, in 1982, Mel Brooks was a safe bet.

Margaret Butler had seen *Young Frankenstein* five times already, but she didn't mind seeing it again. As president of the Computer Club, Margaret was the official leader of the computer hackers at Berkeley. She herself, however, was not a hacker. She was just a normal student who happened to be president of a club full of computer addicts. This explained both her unusually attractive appearance—clean hair, fresh face, sexy dress—and the unique status she was about to achieve as the first Computer Club president in recent memory to actually graduate. Her predecessors had all been too busy in the terminal room to keep up their grades.

What was most unusual about Margaret, however, was the research project she was involved with. She was one of a handful of students then working for a junior professor in a cramped office at the rear of the Computer Science Building on a newly begun attempt to program intelligence into a computer—specifically, into a VAX 11/780 minicomputer named Kim. This is what's known as artificial intelligence—AI for short. The hackers thought it a little weird, but none of them actually held it against her.

There was something ironic about their attitude, for it was in an AI lab—the AI lab at MIT—that the hacker subculture had been born. Twenty years ago, when computers were rare and precious machines, a group of computer freaks had coalesced around an assortment of research projects known collectively as Project MAC. (The acronym is said to have stood for any number of things: Machine-Aided Cognition, Man Against Computers, Maniacs and Clowns.) Many of these people later gravitated toward the school's fledgling AI laboratory. By 1965, when the lab moved into its anonymous-looking high-rise on Technology Square, the hackers had taken over the machines. Gradually they evolved into a mutant subculture, a brotherhood in thrall to the computer—and particularly to the notion that the computer should be given the gift of reason.

Their emergence was not without controversy, especially in the popular press. "Computer Elitists Are Seen As Growing Danger," warned the *Chicago Tribune*; "Critics Fear Computers Could Dominate Lives." Beneath the horror-movie headlines, however, lay a deeper, simmering doubt. Several years ago, in a book called *Computer Power and Human Reason,* an MIT professor named Joseph Weizenbaum—himself an AI researcher and a onetime hacker—compared the compulsive programmers of the AI lab to compulsive gamblers. Both, he argued, are suffering from a psychopathology marked by megalomania and fantasies of omnipotence. "The compulsive programmer," he wrote, "is merely the proverbial mad scientist who has been given a theater, the computer, in which he can and does play out his fantasies."

But that was another age. If the hackers at MIT were mad scientists, the hackers at Berkeley were just kids, introverted college students who were lured into computer science by the promise of jobs, only to find themselves seduced by the machines. They were a new breed of hacker, a new generation in a new computer environment. AI was less appealing to them than other, more practical forms of programming. But they liked Margaret all the same.

One reason for that was the work she'd done to make them respectable. The Berkeley Computer Club had been founded by some individuals who went on to make major contributions in computer science—people like Ken Thompson, who was looking for a way to write chess-playing programs at Bell Labs when he came up with UNIX, the computer operating system that has since become standard among academic researchers. But the club itself had always had a reputation for frivolity. It was an open secret, for example, that most people joined only to get free access to the university computer system—something club members get in exchange for tutoring other students. They use these accounts to play games like Adventure and Rogue for days at a time.

It was Margaret who led them in the transformation from a "club" to an "association"—the Computer Science Undergraduate Association, which was now their official name. The change had done wonders. As a club, they'd been seen as a bunch of computer crazies out to have fun; as an association, they could claim status as a legitimate organization representing computer students in the general free-for-all that is undergraduate life at Berkeley. It didn't hurt that their new acronym, CSUA, was unwieldy enough to be taken seriously by the administration.

That night at Wheeler, though, the organization was functioning in its alter ego as the Computer Club. Everyone was a little punch-drunk. It was Friday evening, and the temporary relief from academic pressure had left them in a state of silly animation. Margaret, looking like a blond Claudette Colbert with her bobbed hair and demure gray dress, was sitting in the middle of the core group of hackers, eight or ten puffy-looking young men in cord pants and plaid shirts. They were reminiscing about some of the other things the Computer Club had done—last month's Dungeons and Dragons tournament . . . the quarterly game of Killer, which gives students a chance to stalk each other in hunt-and-kill mode until only one is left "alive" . . . the annual Hacker's Ball, which was held last year in a senior citizens' center . . . the hot-tub parties . . .

Wait a minute. The guy on Margaret's left hadn't heard about any hot-tub parties. "I've never even been to one of the Hacker's Balls," he declared.

"I've been to every three of them," the student next to him said proudly.

"*All* three of them," another student put in.

Margaret grinned. "Also, computer students don't know how to speak," she said.

"English is my favorite language," the student beside her declared. "It's the only one I know."

"I know Pascal," Margaret said. "And I know FORTRAN and know—"

"Those aren't *languages!*"

"Did you see the ad in the *Daily Cal* today? The *Daily Cal* is looking for people for the CIA—computer scientists and engineers. And the languages they're accepting are Russian et cetera et cetera, and I thought, Hey, as a computer scientist I can go to Russia and translate into FORTRAN. I can translate Russian Pascal into English Pascal!"

Suddenly the lights went down and the curtain rose. Everyone grew quiet. Mr. Bill appeared on the screen. Mr. Bill was the hapless little clay figure on "Saturday Night Live," the one who's forever being victimized by the wicked Sluggo and mangled by an omnipotent pair of human hands—his creator. In the first short, Mr. Bill goes to a psychiatrist—a certain Dr. Hands—who tells him he's paranoid and gives him a lobotomy with a pair of scissors. In the second, Mr. Bill decides to get even and ends up in jail; his wife has an affair with Warden Sluggo, and Mr. Hands helps him escape with a lighted stick of dynamite. There was a message here: Don't be a victim. These people had already gotten it. That's why they were computer students.

Young Frankenstein was different. This was pure fun—Mel Brooks milking one of Western civilization's great horror stories for laughs. Frizzy-haired, baby-faced Gene Wilder plays Professor Frankenstein, the thoroughly American grandson of the mad scientist whose experiments in artificial revivification earned him lasting notoriety. When we first meet him, Frankenstein is justifiably ashamed of his family heritage. But then he is lured to his

4

grandfather's castle, and soon he and his hunchbacked handyman, Igor ("My grandfather used to work for your grandfather," Igor had said by way of introduction), are out robbing a graveyard. Frankenstein unknowingly stitches a defective brain into the corpse and then sets out to bestow life upon his handiwork. "He's hideous," says his lab assistant, the buxom Inga. "He's beautiful," says Frankenstein, "and he's mine."

Slowly Frankenstein is raised on a platform to the top of the tower from which he will direct the massive charge of electricity that will animate his creation. "From that fateful day when stinking bits of slime first crawled from the sea and shouted to the cold stars *'I am man!'* " he screams, in a soliloquy that parodies the lure of science, "our greatest dread has been the knowledge of our own mortality. But tonight, we shall hurl the gauntlet of science into the frightful face of death itself! Tonight we shall enter the heavens! We shall mock the earthquake! We shall command the thunderheads and penetrate *into the very womb of nature herself!*" And then, as the wind howls and the lightning flashes and the thunderclaps peal and electricity arcs into the machinery below, Frankenstein, quite berserk now, shrieks, *"Life! Life,* do you hear me! *Give my creation—LIIIIFE!"*

Meanwhile, in the town below, the local peasants have gathered to discuss the strange behavior of the castle's new occupant. These people are justifiably nervous; it has happened before, after all. Finally one of their number can contain his fears no longer. "He's a Frankenstein," the man shouts, "and they're all alike! It's in their blood! They can't help it! All those scientists, all alike! They say they're working for us, but what they really want is *to rule the world!"*

It's an old argument, as ludicrous in the Mel Brooks version as it had been compelling in Mary Shelley's original. Why would anyone want to tamper with the natural order of things? What is it that makes a scientist want to play God when the consequences of error could be so dear? What is the lure of the forbidden task? This was what had bothered the eighteen-year-old wife of Percy Shelley that cold, wet summer of 1816, when she and Shelley and Byron and his physician, housebound all, had gathered by the fire in a Swiss villa to trade ghost stories.

Byron had rented this house on the shores of Lake Geneva to

get away from England, where the abandonment of his wife and his infant daughter, Ada, for an incestuous liaison with his half sister had created a public outrage; but the constant rains prevented any possibility of recreation. It had been Byron's idea to entertain themselves by telling stories, and it is one of the minor ironies of literature that it was not his or Shelley's tales that would be remembered but Mary's—for hers was the one that would tap a nerve.

She did it not with a monster story—that aspect would be highlighted much later, in the movie versions—but with the narrative of a young man whose megalomaniac ambitions have driven him to play God. The myth of Prometheus was much on their minds that summer: Byron was writing his *Prometheus,* Shelley was only a couple of years away from beginning his lyrical drama *Prometheus Unbound,* and so it should not be surprising that Mary's story itself would be subtitled *The Modern Prometheus* when it was published two years later.

In Greek legend, Prometheus was the Titan who shaped mankind and gave him the gift of fire. Zeus punished him for this presumptuousness by chaining him to a rock and sending an eagle to peck his liver; he punished humanity by sending Pandora, whose curiosity would unleash the evils of the world. But while Shelley and Byron were champions of Prometheanism—the noble yearning to create, to quest, to reach beyond one's grasp—Mary clearly had a different view. Her novel was a monstrous "What if?"—what if the modern Prometheus made a clumsy miscalculation, or failed to measure up to the moral demands of his task, or lacked a true understanding of his quest? The results, she averred in *Frankenstein,* would not be pleasant to consider.

Of course, all this was far from the minds of Margaret and the hackers as they sat in the Wheeler auditorium laughing at the antics of Gene Wilder and his monster sidekick. And yet they were issues she'd have to deal with again next Monday, when she returned to the little room in Evans where the artificial intelligence group has its office.

1

Berkeley

Evans Hall is a building with a powerful presence: a temple of mathematics and computer science in the form of a massive concrete bunker bigger than anything else on campus. It can be seen from miles away, its immense bulk resting solid against the Berkeley Hills. Closer up, it recedes into the background, becomes the background, an all-encompassing entity approached across a featureless plaza that leads to a series of blank glass doors. To enter it is to step into the world of the number and its machine: chilly, gray, exciting, the future.

The fifth-floor lounge in Evans is a respite of sorts, a warren for humans fitted out with trimly modern furniture done in friendly hardwoods and brightly colored fabrics. Directly outside the window lies the Golden Gate, a distant gap between the hills of San Francisco and the rugged headlands to the north. San Francisco is a city of the senses. Lucre or lust—which vice to pursue? That had been the question since Gold Rush days and was the question still, the champions of finance finding their answer in the sleek skyscrapers downtown, the partisans of the flesh finding theirs in the rum-dum seediness of the Tenderloin or in the shadowy recesses of Folsom Street, where warehousemen work by day. Berkeley, rising in the foreground, is different. Berkeley is a city of the mind.

A college town from the beginning, it was laid out in the post–

Civil War years by the founders of the University of California. Its name was a tribute to Bishop Berkeley, the eighteenth-century immaterialist philosopher. (He thought the world consisted of nothing but ideas.) Berkeley was an early proponent of education for "aboriginal Americans," by which he meant Indians. "Westward the course of empire takes its way," he'd written in a poetic treatise entitled "On the Prospect of Planting Arts and Learning in America." That was exactly what the founders had in mind. Led by Henry Durant, a Christian missionary from Yale,* these Victorian gentlemen had fled the roughneck temptations of nearby Oakland to establish in the wilderness an Athens of the Pacific, a city of learning whose lamp would light the way for mankind. At one point they even considered naming the hills and streams after those in the original Athens—Ilissus, Hymettus, and so forth. Eventually, however, they settled for a simpler scheme, naming the north-south streets after contemporary scientists and the east-west streets after men of letters.

Berkeley today is a jumble of concrete superimposed upon a Maxfield Parrish vision of education. The vision is pure: Inspired by the generosity of Phoebe Hearst, the widow of millionaire senator George Hearst and mother of newspaper magnate William Randolph Hearst, the University went on a building spree at the turn of the century that transformed it into a monument to learning in the Columbian Empire. Grand edifices of marble and granite took shape among the eucalyptus groves, and the name of Hearst was everywhere enshrined—Hearst Mining Building, Hearst Gymnasium, Hearst Stadium, Hearst Avenue. The Blue and Gold—that was Yale blue and California gold, President Benjamin Ide Wheeler explained in 1901—carried the Hearst banner high against rivaling Stanford, the private university founded on the ranch of California's other millionaire senator, Leland Stanford. Eventually, however, the Hearst generosity expired; at the same time, the pressures of a rapidly growing population transformed the university into a vast and impersonal behemoth—

---

*California in Gold Rush days was still the sort of place that attracted missionaries. It must not have been too far removed from the age of Porsches and hot tubs, however, for the Reverend Durant described the inhabitants as "sensualists and materialists" and observed, "Our fast living may almost all of it be referred to intense selfishness."

nine campuses, more than 130,000 students. And so, not surprisingly, budget constraints have given recent construction a pinched and angry air. Instead of columns and balustrades, there is plate glass and concrete; in place of graciousness, there is harsh utilitarianism.

Certainly utilitarian is the word for Evans, a building whose most striking internal features are its air-conditioning shafts, vast ten-story pits of raw gray concrete put there to keep the computers from overheating. It sits in the northeast corner of the campus —an area dominated by the engineering school, an area set off from the liberal arts zone by a sort of invisible psychic barrier. Directly beneath it is a row of ramshackle World War II "temporary buildings" nestled inconspicuously in a hemlock grove. There are six of them, unceremoniously labeled T–4 through T–9, each one slowly decaying into the soil. The spot where Evans now stands once held T–1, T–2, and T–3. Evans went up about a decade ago and is not considered an improvement, aesthetically speaking.

The interiors of Evans look like the interiors of power plants and weapons labs—spare, no-nonsense, designed for control. Such a room is the fifth-floor lounge. Normally this is a place where graduate students and faculty members in the computer science division of the electrical engineering department can sit around, drink coffee, and talk over their work. But on a Thursday afternoon in March, due to a scheduling conflict, it had been pressed into temporary service as a classroom for a graduate seminar in artificial intelligence. The professor was Robert Wilensky, thirty, a dynamic individual who'd arrived four years earlier from Yale.

Though he was sitting in the background, stretched out across an armchair, there was no doubt that Wilensky was the dominant presence in the room. Tall and lanky, he looked less like a college professor than like a Silicon Valley electronics executive. He didn't seem distracted or given to cultivating his eccentricities. Even while relaxing, he managed to look like a man in a hurry. He wore his hair in a modish cut, full and over the ears. His clothes were casual but not scruffy: beige slacks, V-neck sweater, pinstripe shirt, open collar. His speech was rapid-fire and nasal without sounding harsh—Brooklyn with an Ivy League patina and a California overlay. Ten years at Yale had smoothed out the rough spots, and four years at Berkeley had rounded off the edges, but nothing could obliterate a Jewish childhood in Brooklyn.

Wilensky had grown up in an Orthodox household on Avenue Z, in an out-of-the-way neighborhood known as Sheepshead Bay. His mother had come from Rumania, his father's father from the Russian province of Bessarabia. His father had never finished high school. But Bob had been both rebellious and a math whiz, and in 1968 he became the second graduate of Sheepshead Bay High School to go off to an Ivy League college. Now, fourteen years later, with a Ph.D. in computer science, he was creating an artificial intelligence lab at one of the major universities of the world.

Every week, one of his grad students would give a talk, either on his own research or on that of someone else whose approach might be relevant. Today the speaker was Yigal Arens, a thirty-year-old Israeli who was working toward a doctorate in artificial intelligence. His talk was on MOPs—Memory Organization Packets, a concept that might or might not prove useful in the transfer of intelligence from human to machine.

The students settled down slowly. There were seven of them, counting Arens; all but Margaret were grad students. Blue jeans and T-shirts were the standard dress, although one person stood out rather markedly. That was Joe Faletti, a bearded, dark-haired young man with a penchant for polyester in exuberant hues. Aside from Wilensky, he and Arens were the oldest people in the room; both had been grad students at Berkeley for eight years, having started out in mathematics and worked their way toward artificial intelligence. The others were more recent arrivals—a math graduate from Brown, a philosophy major from Columbia, a math grad from Harvard, a computer student from MIT. All were part of Wilensky's government-funded research team, Berkeley Artificial Intelligence Research—BAIR for short.

Somebody mentioned Jerry Brown, who'd been on campus the day before to address a conference the engineering school was holding on its industrial-liaison program. In his final year as governor, Brown had discovered the economic importance of high technology; he'd come to Berkeley to urge industry to invest in research and education so California could remain competitive with Japan and Korea and other countries on the Pacific rim. Wilensky had come away from Brown's talk with new hope for artificial intelligence. "You can really believe that computers can think if you see that guy," he told his students with a grin. "There's no spark of humanity in him at all."

Yigal stood up to begin. He didn't look any more like an academic than Wilensky did. He looked like a cleaned-up guerrilla from the Middle East. He was dressed entirely in blue denim, with salt-and-pepper hair curling well below his collar. He had a three-day growth of beard, and on his right hip, attached to his belt, was a brown leather pouch that looked like it was supposed to hold hand grenades, or perhaps a snub-nosed revolver. In fact, however, the pouch held only pens and a wallet, and the beard was more the product of a lingering aversion to shaving than anything else. The blue denim just happened to be his standard uniform.

Slowly, deliberately, Yigal handed out a four-page computer printout to the students gathered around him. The printout contained the outline for his talk. It was filled with phrases like "data structures" and "memory node" and "planlike formulations." He gave a little smile and started talking about something he called "scripts." There was a problem with scripts, he said. MOPs had been designed to solve it.

Like Wilensky, MOPs had come from Yale. The idea had been developed by Roger Schank, the head of the AI effort there, as part of his general theory of understanding.

A very large part of the task of getting computers to "think"— as opposed to using them to blindly manipulate symbols such as words or numbers, which is what computers have been used for from the beginning—involves getting them to "understand." But what is meant by *understanding,* and whether computers are capable of doing it, and how someone would know if they ever succeeded—all these are the subject of intense and continuing debate.

In essence, understanding is the ability to make sense of the world—to organize data in a meaningful way. In *Scripts, Plans, Goals and Understanding,* the book he wrote with social psychologist Robert Abelson, Schank defines it as "a process by which people match what they see and hear to [that which] they have already experienced." In other words, understanding is the ability to match symbols with other symbols and with the concepts they represent—to match *bread* with bread, for example, or *automobile* with a particular car on the street. But that still leaves unanswered the question of *levels* of understanding, not to mention the matter of how understanding actually works and whether it can occur in inanimate objects such as computers.

The problem of understanding understanding is really part of the larger problem of the mind understanding itself—and that's only half of what AI researchers like Schank and Wilensky are trying to do. AI research is actually a highly specialized form of computer programming. A program is a series of coded instructions to the machine. A computer can be programmed to do anything that can be expressed in a precise and unambiguous set of instructions—what's known in computer science as an "algorithm." A computer, then, can do anything you can program it to do; without a program, it can do nothing at all. What AI researchers try to do is write programs that enable computers to think for themselves.

Schank is known for his commitment to the "cognitive modeling" approach to AI. The idea behind cognitive modeling is to develop computer programs that don't just think, but that think in much the same way people do. Schank is hardly the first to try this route—the question of how the mind works was what motivated many AI researchers from the beginning—but it's so central to his work that it's become the defining characteristic of what's now called the "Schankian school" of artificial intelligence. And so at Yale and at Schankian outposts such as Berkeley and Columbia, AI researchers theorize about how people think, much as a psychologist might. But where psychologists attempt to verify their theories by experimenting with human subjects, AI researchers verify theirs by writing a computer program.

One of the problems with this approach is that nobody really knows very much about how the human mind works. We know a few basic facts about the brain. We know that the brain contains at least 100 billion nerve cells, known as "neurons," each one linked to thousands of other neurons by microscopic gaps called "synapses." We know that these neurons, when stimulated, fire electrochemical impulses across these gaps at the rate of a thousand per second. This is what thinking is: the rapid firing of electrochemical transmitters across infinitesimal gaps inside the skull.

We know, too, that there are three distinct regions of the brain and that they correspond to different phases of evolutionary development. There's the "reptilian brain," a primitive lump at the base of the skull that takes care of such instinctive survival functions as sleeping, breathing, and fighting. Surrounding that is the brain of the ancestral mammal, which evolved some 100 million years ago to handle such emotions as anger, love and fear. And finally there's a much larger outer layer, the cerebrum, that's responsible for most conscious thought. We used to think that in most people the left side of the cerebrum took care of linear and analytical types of thought—logic, language, mathematics—and the right side handled holistic processes such as aesthetics and creativity, but recent findings have cast even that theory in doubt. And we still don't know how memory works, or even where it is located. For that matter, we have only recently concluded that what we call "mind" is really the activity of the brain —what the brain *does*— rather than some immaterial phenomenon that exists independently of the body.

We are, in short, still largely in the dark. Our position has been compared to that of an electrical engineer who has never seen a television before and is expected to explain its inner workings, not by going inside and tearing it apart but by studying the signals it receives and what comes out on the screen. We have no way to experience the electrochemical excitation of our neurons. We know the mind by what it produces—language, vision, consciousness, thought. We know the input and the output, but very little of the processing in between.

With computers, the situation is exactly the opposite—the processing is all we know. Programmers can trace a function with a tap on the keyboard. Serious computer hackers can translate a program into machine language—zeros and ones—and tell you how it works on the binary level. Circuit designers can follow the blip of electrons through the microscopic maze of a silicon chip. But the input and the output of intelligent behavior—those are the questions. What goes into it? And how do you know it when you see it?

Another problem with the cognitive modeling approach is that the kind of things that are easiest for humans to do—such as recognizing a friend on the street, or understanding one's native language—are precisely the things that are most difficult for computers. Artificial-intelligence researchers have been much more successful at getting computers to display intelligence in areas that humans can master only with a lot of effort, areas such as medicine or geology.

Researchers at Stanford, for example, have developed a program called MYCIN that diagnoses certain types of blood infections, and another called DENDRAL that deduces the structure of molecules and their atomic constituents from data provided by mass spectrometers, which are used by chemists to break molecules apart. Researchers at SRI International, a high-technology think tank in the neighboring town of Menlo Park, have been working since 1976 on PROSPECTOR, a program designed to locate underground mineral deposits. MIT has a program called MACSYMA that solves the kind of complex mathematical problems a theoretical physicist is liable to encounter. All these are examples of what are known in the trade as "expert systems"— computer programs with enough knowledge to display intelligence in a certain highly technical field. The main thing that sets them apart from other artificial-intelligence programs is their usefulness.

From its inception, artificial intelligence has been regarded as a blue-sky endeavor—the kind of activity that might eventually produce results but could hardly be expected to pay off in any bottom-line sense. For that reason, work in this area has been conducted almost exclusively in university labs and funded almost exclusively by the federal government. Most of the money has come from the Pentagon.

The success of expert systems, however, has suddenly made AI a paying concern. In the past few years, AI "start-up" firms have proliferated in California and Massachusetts, and a number of major corporations have fielded serious research teams of their own. Xerox and Texas Instruments are working on programs that will help design computer chips, whose ever-shrinking circuitry is becoming too complex for the human mind to comprehend. IBM and DEC (Digital Equipment Corporation, the leading manufacturer of minicomputers) are each developing programs that will spot the trouble with malfunctioning computers much the way intelligent-doctor programs diagnose human illnesses. Schlumberger, the multinational conglomerate that dominates the oil-field services business, has developed the prototype for a highly specialized system that will analyze drilling-site data to determine if a site is likely to bear oil.

As futuristic as all these programs sound, they're actually quite limited. Computers will never be truly intelligent as long as they know about only one subject, no matter how useful the subject or impressive their command of it. Computers won't be truly intelligent until they know as much as humans do—and don't just know it in the sense having a lot of symbols stored in a data base, but understand it as well.

For much of the past decade, Schank has been trying to demonstrate a computer's capacity to understand by writing programs that can digest a story and then answer questions about it, using information that's not actually in the story. This is the ability to make inferences—one facet of understanding. Schank and his students, Wilensky among them, have written a variety of programs that exhibit it.

Several years ago, a number of these programs were hooked together to form a single large system known as BORIS—Better Organized Reasoning and Inference System. Among other things, BORIS knows a lot about what motivates people and how they behave in restaurants. Informed that an imaginary human named George was having lunch when a waitress knocked a glass of Coke into his lap, and that George then got upset and left without paying his check, BORIS was able to make responses that suggested genuine comprehension:

Q: Why did the waitress spill the Coke on George?
A: She did it by accident.
Q: Did George pay at the restaurant?
A: No. The waitress had given George bad service.

Other programs developed by students at Yale specialize in digesting information that appears in the news. A program called IPP, for example, follows news stories about terrorism and learns from them. IPP's special talent is the ability to make generalizations: Italian terrorists tend to kidnap businessmen; IRA terrorists are more likely to send letter bombs. An earlier program, FRUMP, skimmed wire-service stories on all sorts of subjects and provided terse, one-sentence summaries in English, Russian, or Spanish. It ran into trouble, however, with the report that the shooting of the mayor of San Francisco "shook" the city; taking the word literally, it announced that California had suffered an earthquake.

One of Schank's earliest story-understander programs was called SAM, for Script-Applier Mechanism. It was his view at the time that we go through life with a standard set of expectations for such everyday experiences as going to a restaurant or a movie or a supermarket. These expectations he called "scripts." When we enter a restaurant, according to this theory, we subconsciously refer to a restaurant script, which tells us what to do. We know we're supposed to sit down and wait for a waiter who'll ask us what we'd like and come back with the food we ordered—food that we're then expected to eat and pay for. When we go to McDonald's, we use a fast-food variant of the restaurant script, which tells us that none of this will happen if we simply sit down —that we have to go to the counter to order our food and pay for it and then take it to a table and eat it. It was scripts that enabled BORIS to understand why George walked out of the restaurant without paying.

Before coming up with his script idea, Schank had developed a system for reducing normal English, with its myriad complexities and ambiguities, to something a computer could understand. This notation, which he called "conceptual dependency" because it deals with elemental concepts and their relations to, or dependencies on, each other, offers a systematic method of eliminating the more troublesome aspects of ordinary language.

From an AI programmer's point of view, the problem with English or any other natural language—as opposed to computer languages like BASIC or FORTRAN—is its frustrating ambiguity. A single word or phrase can mean any number of different things, depending on the context. Sentences can have a similar structure but vastly different meanings—"John shot the girl with a rifle" as opposed to "John shot the girl with long hair," to pick an example from a paper Schank wrote years ago. Or they can mean the same thing but be stated differently—"I like books," "Books please me." In conceptual dependency, any two sentences that mean the same thing would be represented the same way. By focusing on meaning rather than on structure—on semantics rather than on syntax—the underlying meaning can be made evident.

Schank's conceptual-dependency scheme works by reducing all acts to one of eleven basic primitives. These he has given names like "ATrans," "PTrans," "MBuild," and "Speak." Each primitive has a broad meaning that erases the subtle distinctions of hundreds of English verbs. *ATrans* means giving or taking or buying—that is, the transfer of anything abstract, such as possession or control. *PTrans* includes such actions as walking or riding or going or putting—anything that refers to the physical transfer of an object. *MTrans* is used for the transfer of mental concepts —that is, information—through talking, writing, and so forth. *MBuild* means processing information—in other words, thinking. *Speak* means producing sounds, whether by talking or shrieking. *Attend* means paying attention with the eyes or the ears. *Ingest* includes eating and drinking. And so on, until every act that can be expressed in English has been reduced to one of these primitive concepts. Until, in other words, we PTrans ourselves to a restaurant instead of going to it; we MTrans our order to the waiter instead of giving it to him; and instead of paying for our meal, we ATrans some money to the cashier. It may not be the stuff of poetry, but it is an unambiguous way of representing meaning.

Representing meaning, most AI researchers now feel, is the key to computer intelligence. This task is known in the jargon of the trade as "knowledge representation." It means defining and organizing the vast amount of knowledge we humans have at our disposal—both the complex, highly sophisticated knowledge we generally associate with intelligence and the ordinary, everyday sort of knowledge we call "common sense." Early AI research concentrated on the use of sophisticated knowledge—mathematics, for example. Common sense is so basic to human experience and human functioning that hardly anyone thought to examine it until recently. But together with language, it seems to define the essence of what it means to be human. Communicating this essence to computers is what the AI effort at Berkeley is all about.

This is a complex undertaking. It requires taking the sum of human experience—thousands of years of accumulated knowledge about the world and how it works—and rewriting it step by step in computer code. It means organizing that code in such a way that the computer not only can manipulate the data it has been given but can also understand it and learn from it. And it raises a number of unanswered questions—unanswered and possibly unanswerable.

Can human experience actually be formalized in this way? Can a computer's electronic circuitry "understand" the way a living brain does? If so, does that mean a computer could become imbued with consciousness? And what would be the consequences of that—of introducing nonliving yet intelligent beings onto our planet? Could a silicon-based intelligence turn out to be, as some scientists have predicted, the next step on the evolutionary ladder? And if so, how do we know that a new race of vastly more intelligent machines would act in our interest?

But perhaps these questions are premature. All that is certain right now is that the development of the digital calculating machine has set us on a path from which there is no turning back. The Promethean quest for knowledge is self-generating and unstoppable. At the moment, human researchers are still in the very early stages of this particular quest. But you have to start somewhere, and this afternoon at Berkeley we were starting with MOPs.

Memory Organization Packets, Yigal Arens was explaining in the fifth-floor lounge, came about because recent developments have cast some doubt on the validity of the script idea as a model for human memory. Scripts were originally intended to serve both as a basis for expectations—what would you expect to happen in a given situation?—and as a basis for memory structure—how should a given piece of information be stored? Now, however, Schank has concluded that memory can't really be explained in terms of calling up a series of stereotypical situations. He has decided that scripts were all wrong.

The main problem with scripts was their inflexibility. They weren't flexible enough to explain human behavior, nor were they general enough to explain how we adjust to new situations. Besides, there would have to be millions of scripts to explain all the different situations we're liable to find ourselves in. Also, people sometimes get their stereotypical situations confused—something that wouldn't happen if each script were a discrete entity. Gordon Bower, a psychologist at Stanford, tested Schank's script idea and found that people confused stories that happened in doctors' offices with stories that happened in dentists' offices. "Why do people confuse the doctor script and the dentist script?" Yigal asked. "Maybe because it's a general visit-health-professional script?"

And so Schank has come up with a somewhat more sophisticated theory that addresses these problems. This time he has arbitrarily divided memory into several different levels. The lowest level is "event memory," which contains the details of specific events and which decays over time until all we're left with is the unusual features of those events. Then there's "generalized event memory," which contains the common features of events that have happened several times. Above that there's "situational memory," which contains information about situations we find ourselves in frequently. And finally there's "intentional memory," which contains the rules we use for getting things done—buying an airline ticket, for example. All these memories are contained in various "memory organization packets," which can be reached in a number of different ways. And instead of scripts, we use "superscripts," which are constructed as needed from the information contained in different MOPs.

In this scheme, then, being reminded of something consists of finding the highest-level memory—event, generalized event, situational, or intentional—that matches the situation you're in at the moment. Understanding something consists of using that memory to figure out what to expect next. "Say you go to a fast-food restaurant," Yigal explained. "You've only been to McDonald's. But you walk into a Burger King and you recognize that you're in a similar situation. That way you know you have to walk up to the counter and order your food, rather than taking a seat and giving your order to a waiter."

No one spoke as Yigal went through his presentation. Only occasionally did anyone jot something down. The Berkeley group was working on its own ways of organizing memory, and there was no point in taking notes unless something came up they could borrow. Wilensky sat in the background and said nothing.

When Yigal finished, however, Wilensky took over, and suddenly the seminar shifted from a neutral and somewhat tentative description of Schank's latest knowledge-representation scheme to a spirited and rapid-fire evaluation of its faults and virtues— mostly the former. "This is a theory I don't like too much," Wilensky declared. "Two things are confused here. Memory—how do you use it to make associations?—and representation—how do you represent complex things? Everything you want to access for memory you have to build a node for. If you don't build a node for it when it happens, there's no way to access it later."

In the brain, nodes are fibers in the neurons that pass electrochemical impulses from one neuron to another. In AI programs, nodes are "pointers"—pieces of memory structure that point to other pieces of memory structure. Wilensky felt that with MOPs, Schank had focused too much on how these nodes should be set up and not enough on how they should work.

"Roger asked the right question," he continued, "which is how things are associated in memory. It's a very Schankian theory in this sense—a theory of particular keys that remind you of things. But it was created to address the problem of how two different things seem to be similar, and it ended up being a theory of nodes you should organize memory around."

Outside, the clock on the Campanile read 3:30. The seminar was over. MOPs, it seemed, were not the answer.

2

The Machine

In the spring of 1982, Robert Wilensky was one of several hundred individuals in the United States with a Ph.D. in artificial intelligence. He was the only such person at Berkeley. Through a mixture of politics and oversight, California's massive "superuniversity"—the most impressive agglomeration of academic brainpower in the country, according to the latest rankings—had managed for two decades to avoid the field almost entirely. A young Carnegie Tech graduate named Edward Feigenbaum had tried to start an AI program in the early Sixties, but organizational disputes and institutional indifference soon encouraged him to depart for Stanford, where he became a pioneer in expert systems —applied AI, or, as Feigenbaum calls it, "knowledge engineering." An Iranian-American mathematician named Lotfi Zadeh has been an interested observer but has never attempted to mount a research effort. That role awaited the arrival of Wilensky in the fall of 1978.

At that point, the pursuit of artificial intelligence in America was little more than two decades old. AI officially began with the Dartmouth Conference, called in 1956 by John McCarthy, then a Dartmouth mathematics professor, and Marvin Minsky, then a junior fellow at Harvard. Minsky and McCarthy, together with Nathaniel Rochester, an information specialist at IBM, and Claude Shannon, an information specialist at AT&T, got a $7,500 grant from the Rockefeller Foundation that year for a ten-man summer conference to discuss the almost unheard-of idea "that every aspect of learning or any other feature of intelligence can in principle be so precisely described that a machine can be made to simulate it." It was at Dartmouth, at McCarthy's urging, that the term *artificial intelligence* was adopted, and it was at Dartmouth that the first genuinely intelligent computer program was demonstrated—the Logic Theorist of Allen Newell and Herbert Simon, two researchers associated with the Rand Corporation and with Pittsburgh's Carnegie Tech, as Carnegie-Mellon University was then known. These four men—Minsky, McCarthy, Newell, and Simon—directed most of the significant AI research in the United States for the next twenty years, and the schools they settled at—MIT, Stanford, and Carnegie-Mellon—continue to dominate the field today.

By the time Wilensky left for Berkeley, however, the pursuit of artificial intelligence had spread far beyond those three schools. Major research programs were under way at Brown, at Edinburgh, at IBM, at Fairchild, at universities and think tanks and corporate laboratories around the globe. Yale was beginning to emerge as an especially potent force in the AI community, thanks to the efforts of Roger Schank, a brash, hard-driving young man who'd come there from Stanford. The San Francisco Bay Area had the largest concentration of AI research facilities anywhere: two labs at Stanford—Feigenbaum's Heuristic Programming Project and John McCarthy's Stanford Artificial Intelligence Laboratory, otherwise known as SAIL—and others at SRI International (the former Stanford Research Institute), Fairchild Semiconductor, and Xerox PARC (for Palo Alto Research Center). All of these were clustered around the Peninsula suburb of Palo Alto, twenty-five miles south of San Francisco. Berkeley had not been heard from.

The explanation was curiously human. For years, computer science at Berkeley had been dominated by theorists, brilliant individuals who'd made names for themselves in pursuit of the fundamental limits of computation. People in theory are interested in the deep philosophical questions of mathematics. For them, the computer is a tool. They tend not to care about such frivolous concerns as whether it can think.

To the extent that computer scientists at Berkeley did think about AI, they were likely to consider it suspect—for despite its wildly futuristic potential, AI is viewed as an application of computer science, and applications are never as highly regarded as pure science. The irony is that many academics regard computer science itself as a suspect discipline. Mathematicians consider the whole thing an application. Scientists view anything that smacks of engineering with disdain. And computer science is a branch of engineering, though the exact relationship is so cloudy that the field is liable to turn up almost anywhere on an organizational chart. Should it be a subdomain of electrical engineering? An engineering discipline in its own right? A liberal arts/engineering hybrid? Any decision can only be regarded as arbitrary.

Historically, computer science is a fusion of mathematics and electrical engineering, which is itself an outgrowth of physics. Electrical engineering deals with certain technologically useful properties of the electron. Its products are the microchip, the microwave, the laser beam, the information technologies behind the information age. These technologies have created a new commodity—"information," or digitally encoded data—that is as essential as coal or oil, but invisible and without substance. It has put us on the threshold of a new world, a rapidly emerging postindustrial world in which brainpower is amplified by electronics the way musclepower was amplified by the machines of the Industrial Revolution. This is the world in which intelligent machines are a possibility.

But computer science is also an outgrowth of mathematics, and in that sense it isn't really an engineering discipline at all. In that sense, computer science is the study of computation and computing machinery. Of its several subdomains—computational theory, software design, data-base management (data bases are computerized information banks), artificial intelligence, computer architecture and design—only the last requires any real knowledge of how electrons behave. The theoretical side of computer science actually predates the invention of the computer by several decades. Most of the rest of it consists of different types of programming —an activity that resembles writing in that it's done at a keyboard, and engineering in its reliance on mathematical precision. Unlike writing, however, programming doesn't produce anything humans can read; and unlike engineering, it doesn't produce anything they can hold in their hands or plug into the wall or ride to the moon.

At Berkeley, computer science is a division of the department of electrical engineering and computer science. Berkeley's electrical engineering department is one of the best in the world. Its computer science division, despite the presence of several brilliant theorists, was until recently something of a bureaucratic stepchild. One of its chief problems was that it didn't have much in the way of computers. There were some antiquated machines for undergraduate instruction—that much could be said of computer science departments everywhere. But the computing power for research wasn't impressive either. There was a well-known data-base management project that had some serious resources, but very little was available to the random researcher who simply had a bright idea. And so, unlike Stanford or MIT, Berkeley has developed little in the way of a computer culture—no legendary brotherhood, steeped in the lore of the machine; just hordes of calculating undergraduates, eager for a job.

What Berkeley does have are two philosophers who've made it their business to become virulent critics of artificial intelligence. One of them is Hubert Dreyfus, a feisty existentialist who argues, in a book entitled *What Computers Can't Do,* that the whole thing is simply impossible. The other is John Searle, a compelling speaker who's made a name for himself in the philosophical realm of causality. Searle claims that even if artificial intelligence does succeed, it won't matter, because computers will only be able to simulate intelligence, not produce the real thing. When a computer is used to simulate a rainstorm, he points out, nobody gets wet; why should anyone assume that a computer simulation of intelligence would be any more effective?

All these factors put Wilensky in the position of the missionary, bringing an alien religion into the enemy camp—which is precisely what he'd been hired to do.

The theorists had been hearing about artificial intelligence for quite a while, and some of them had decided it was time to get involved. Also, AI requires a lot of computing power—intelligence does not come cheap—and it had occurred to some people that if AI came to Berkeley, computers might follow. The chairman of the division at the time (though a satellite of electrical engineering, computer science at Berkeley does enjoy limited self-government) was Manuel Blum, a numbers man whose specialty is the development of cryptography protocols that would permit electronic business transactions. He was strongly in favor of bringing AI to Berkeley, and he led the search for a young man to make it happen.

"Manuel!" said Wilensky with a grin. "Manuel is my nominee for sainthood, okay?"

Any university starting a new program faces a choice: Whether to hire a senior person in the field, or a young person eager to make a name for himself. Berkeley had decided to hire a young person, and that meant finding a brand-new Ph.D. who could fly solo—who could get funding and form a research group and build a whole operation without guidance from anyone. It meant finding a self-starter.

Blum and his associates interviewed more than a dozen people. Wilensky came out at the top of their list. He had a background in natural-language processing; that was a plus because Berkeley already had a strong data-base-management group, and natural language and data-base management together could give you a computerized information bank that would respond to simple English commands—something sure to be popular with the business community. Wilensky also had a lot of ideas about AI, and he seemed to have the necessary entrepreneurial skills. He was the person Blum wanted.

For his part, Wilensky liked Berkeley because it was warm. He had lived on the East Coast all his life—first Brooklyn, then Yale —and the other jobs he was up for were at Carnegie-Mellon in Pittsburgh and the University of Rochester in upstate New York, neither of which offered much in the way of climate. He was intrigued about the politics of the place as well—the free-speech movement, the antiwar radicalism of the Sixties. But the main thing was that Blum made him feel wanted.

Aside from that, there was the challenge. Carnegie and Rochester were sure shots: Carnegie was one of the leading AI centers of the world, and Rochester had an up-and-coming computer science department with a serious AI effort already under way. All he would have to do at either place was plug himself in. Berkeley was different. Berkeley was a place with enormous potential and not much else. It was a chance to start up an entirely new AI program at a major university. At Carnegie or Rochester, he would always be in the shadow of someone else; at Berkeley it would be his game and his alone. Berkeley was the long shot. "So my feeling," he told me one afternoon as we sat in his office, "was that it was the only shot worth playing."

Shortly after Wilensky arrived, the computer science division got its first all-purpose computer—a VAX 11/780 named Ernie. Its full name was Ernie Co-VAX, *Co-* standing for computer science. Half of it was paid for by a $250,000 grant from the National Science Foundation; the rest came from the university and the Department of Energy. It was installed in a windowless nine-by-twenty-foot room on the fifth floor of Evans with a photograph of Ernie Kovacs on the door.

With its printer and its five disk drives, Ernie stands five feet tall and fourteen feet long. It takes up most of the room. It holds 5 million bytes of data in fast-storage capacity, retrievable in 1/500,000 of a second, and another 1 trillion bytes in secondary-storage capacity, retrievable in $\frac{1}{10}$ to $\frac{1}{60}$ of a second. Its presence was what enabled computer scientists at Berkeley to think about competing in the major leagues.

The biggest hurdle in equipping a computer science facility is getting your first big computer and proving you can do something with it. At Berkeley, Ernie was the first big one. The research proposal that brought it was written by Richard Fateman, a symbolic-math person who had worked on the MACSYMA project at MIT. It was Fateman's idea that Ernie should be available to everybody. And so, a couple of years later, when it became known that the Department of Defense was prepared to invest millions of dollars in a computer school to make it the equivalent of Stanford or MIT or Carnegie-Mellon, people at Berkeley could point to themselves and expect to be listened to.

So another proposal was written by Fateman and Wilensky and several of their colleagues, after a lot of consultation with the more senior members of the faculty. It was addressed to ARPA— the Pentagon's Advanced Research Projects Agency, a little-known arm of the DoD that is charged with exploring and exploiting the military potential of "leading edge" technologies. As part of the bailiwick of the undersecretary of defense for research and engineering, familiarly known as USDR&E, ARPA has overseen the research into a number of exotic applications—high-efficiency lasers to fry enemy targets in space; charged-particle-beam weapons to dematerialize them like the ray guns of science fiction; computer systems designed to ensure military command, control, and communications (C^3) capabilities in a "nuclear environment." It has a long-term interest in artificial intelligence.

ARPA gave Berkeley a contract of $1.6 million annually for two years, with the possibility of renewal, to conduct research in a number of areas of computer science. Shortly after that, computers started stacking up in the halls. The first of these was a VAX 11/780 named, naturally enough, ARPA-VAX. Then came UCB-VAX, a smaller 11/750 unit (UCB stands for University of California at Berkeley), and then came a whole series of 11/750s named after artists—Calder, Dali, Matisse, and so on, until by 1983 there would be twenty-six computers linked together in a high-speed network. "The problem," said Fateman, a dark-haired, bespectacled young man who's taken charge of the naming process, "is that we're running out of names. Let's see—the Seven Dwarfs . . . the Seven Deadly Sins . . . that's fourteen. . . ."

One of the machines the ARPA money helped bring in was Kim —Kim No-VAX, so called because Fateman was planning to alter its hardware so that it could no longer technically be considered a VAX. Kim's $175,000 price tag was actually split among ARPA, the Department of Energy (which was paying for Fateman's hardware research), and the Alfred P. Sloan Foundation, a $250-million fund set up by the man who built General Motors. It was installed in the fourth-floor machine room, a cold, windowless space deep in the interior of Evans, a room crowded with VAXes and humming with the vibrations of 2,900 megabytes of electronic data being shuffled and filed.

It is a long room, usually bathed in darkness. The machines are arranged in rows, row after row of trim metal boxes, cables coiled beside them like snakes. Kim is in the first row on the right, by the door. It is a two-tone machine, pale tan body with a light blue top; not as big as Ernie, with only 4 megabytes of fast storage and 600 megabytes of secondary storage, but attractive. On one of its front panels it wears a tiny newspaper photograph of its name-

27

sake, the blond bombshell of the Fifties. In the photograph, Kim Novak appears openmouthed, sultry, expectant. Kim No-VAX gives no such clues to the mysteries within.

One thing we do know about Kim No-VAX is that it's mathematically precise. As a computer, it is an electronic math-and-logic machine that operates on the binary number system. Humans seem innately predisposed to the decimal system, presumably because we come with ten fingers. (The word *digit* is derived from the Latin word for "finger.") Computers have no such proclivity.

Computers work best on the binary system because electronic circuits and binary numbers have something important in common: They have only two possible states—on or off, zero or one. What's more, these two states happen to be directly analogous to the true-or-false possibilities of symbolic logic. It is the congruent behavior of these three elements—electronic circuits, binary mathematics, and symbolic logic—that makes computer thought possible.

Binary numbers work just like decimal numbers, except there are only two of them: 0 and 1. Zero in the binary system is written as 0; one is written as 1. Two, however, is written as 10, because it has a 1 in the twos column and a 0 in the ones column—just as ten is written as 10 in decimal notation because it has a 1 in the *tens* column and a 0 in the ones column. Three in the binary system is written as 11 because it has a 1 in the twos column and a 1 in the ones column, and one 2 and one 1 make three. Four would be written as 100 because it has a 1 in the fours column; five would be 101; six would be 110; seven would be 111; eight would be 1000; and so on. This gets kind of complicated for humans—especially when you get to numbers like 300, which would be written in binary notation as 100101100. But for machines it's simple, because there are only two digits juggled: 0 and 1. What's more, there's no reason these digits have to represent numbers. They are meaningless ciphers which can be strung together to represent anything you want—words, numbers, information, thoughts. Then they become symbols, and computation becomes the process of symbol-manipulation.

Binary number systems antedated the computer by several

thousand years. They weren't used very much, but in the seventeenth century they did attract the attention of the German philosopher/mathematician Gottfried von Leibniz, best remembered today as the inventor of differential calculus. Leibniz also invented a calculating machine that could do arithmetic at the turn of a handle. But the Leibniz calculator worked on the decimal system; its inventor never thought to use binary numbers in machine calculation. His interest in them had more to do with his search for a "universal calculus" by which all of human reason could be reduced to a simple mathematical notation. From this he wandered into an unfortunate attempt to prove that God (1) had created the universe from nothing (0). It was not the right idea.

Leibniz's universal calculus actually was discovered in the nineteenth century by an English mathematician, George Boole. In his *Laws of Thought,* published in 1854, Boole set out to construct "the mathematics of the human intellect"—a formal logic expressed not in words but in unambiguous mathematical symbols. It was his idea that all of logic could be represented as a series of yes-or-no responses, and that these in turn could be expressed in binary terms. The result was an algebra of thought, based on the numbers 0 and 1. It didn't prove anything about God, but (as Douglas Hofstadter pointed out in *Gödel, Escher, Bach*) it did turn out to be the first step toward the creation of a thinking computer program—the software of artificial intelligence.

Computer hardware had its beginnings a couple of decades earlier with the work of another English mathematician, Charles Babbage. The son of a wealthy banker, Babbage was an eccentric and irascible individual, a man who hated street musicians and computational errors with equal intensity. He was also a polymath and a visionary. As an inventor, his contributions included both the cowcatcher and the speedometer. But his best-known invention is one to which he devoted both his life and his fortune without success: A steam-powered computer he called the "analytical engine."

Babbage was not yet thirty when, in 1821, he announced to the Royal Astronomical Society his intention to build an automatic calculating machine he called the Difference Engine. He'd been obsessed with the idea of mechanical calculation for nearly a decade, ever since his mind had wandered off one day as he was poring over a table of logarithms at Cambridge. These tables were filled with mistakes, as were the navigational tables and astronomical charts of the time—a fact that had dire consequences for the sailors who were shipwrecked as a result. Babbage designed his hand-cranked Difference Engine to compute them automatically. The British government supported him with grants that came to £17,000 over the next ten years, but the device was never built, partly because machinists couldn't meet the tolerances required. In 1833 the whole project was suspended with nothing to show but a pile of sprockets and cogwheels in a workshop on Babbage's estate.

Babbage, undeterred, came up with an even grander scheme: his Analytical Engine. Unlike the Difference Engine, which was to have been a special-purpose machine capable only of solving polynomial equations, this new concoction was intended to be a general-purpose computer—the first such device ever conceived. It was to include the three essential elements of any modern computer: a "store" (memory), a "mill" (central processor), and a means of initiating various "patterns of action" (programs). The store and the mill would consist of a clanking assemblage of rods and gears; for programming, Babbage would rely on the same kind of punched cards that were used to control the Jacquard loom, an automatic weaving device that had been invented in France some thirty years before. The resulting contraption, Babbage maintained, would be able to perform calculations at the rate of one per second.

Few people took him seriously. Virtually the only person who did, in fact, was the beautiful young Ada, Countess of Lovelace—Lord Byron's only legitimate daughter. Ada had been born in 1815, the year before Byron left for Switzerland with Shelley and his wife, and she had inherited not her father's poetic romanticism (possibly because she never saw him after her infancy) but her mother's head for mathematics. Taken as a girl to Babbage's workshop to see a model of his Difference Engine, she found herself entranced by its workings. Years later she became his partner in the attempt to bring the Analytical Engine to realization.

But it was not to be. Government funds weren't available this time—Babbage was offered a knighthood instead, but he snubbed it—and he and Lady Lovelace turned to other schemes to raise money: a tic-tac-toe machine, a chess-playing machine, and finally a foolproof system for playing the horses. This last proved quite disastrous, as it resulted in blackmail and twice necessitated the pawning of her husband's family jewels. (Both times her mother bought them back.) Ada died at thirty-six, and with her any chance of the project's completion. Babbage lived on another twenty years, an increasingly embittered old man; after his death his brain was pickled on the off-chance that someone, sometime, would be able to explain its peculiar workings.

That never happened, and Babbage's work was forgotten until well into the next century. A number of calculating machines were produced not long after he died, however—most of them in America, and most of them dependent on two advantages he never had: precision tooling and electricity. The most profitable of these was Herman Hollerith's automatic tabulating machine, an early data processor that was used to great advantage in the 1890 census. Like Babbage's unbuilt engine, the Hollerith tabulator used information supplied by punched cards; each card represented a person, and each punch-hole represented a piece of information about that person and allowed an electrical circuit to be completed that advanced a dial one notch. The success of this device encouraged Hollerith to set up his Tabulating Machine Company, which was bought up by a New York financier and amalgamated into a couple of other companies and reborn in 1924 as IBM. But what he had invented was not a true computer, for it was of little use for anything beyond cataloging piles of data.

It wasn't until the 1930s that the general-purpose computer would be reinvented in theory, and not until the 1940s that it would be realized in fact. The theory was provided by a number of individuals, but perhaps the key contributions were made in two papers, one published in 1936 and the other in 1937, which together can be said to have laid the foundation for the information age. The first was written by a brilliant young Englishman, a Cambridge mathematician named Alan Turing; the other was a master's thesis by an MIT student named Claude Shannon—the same Claude Shannon who nineteen years later joined Minsky and McCarthy in calling for the Dartmouth conference on AI.

Shannon's paper, which he called "A Symbolic Analysis of Relay and Switching Circuits," supplied the link that connected binary math, symbolic logic, and the behavior of electronic circuits. Boolean algebra had demonstrated the connection between mathematics and logic; but like his contemporary Babbage, Boole found that his most important idea drew little attention in his lifetime. Sixty years later, however, Bertrand Russell and Alfred North Whitehead resurrected and perfected it in their *Principia Mathematica,* a three-volume opus that did have some impact. Russell and Whitehead held that logic and mathematics were one—that all questions of logic could be expressed in mathematical terms. Shannon's genius was to see that the same truth applied to electronic circuits—that the propositional calculus of symbolic logic could be used to describe the two-state, on-or-off behavior of an electromechanical relay switch. Yes-no, on-off, true-false, zero-one—it was all the same game. And with this realization came the genesis of what has since come to be known as information theory —the idea that information, like energy or matter, is a quantifiable entity that can be manipulated at will.

Turing's contribution, in a paper entitled "On Computable Numbers," was to create an imaginary computer—a "Turing machine," as it has come to be known—and to demonstrate, in theory, what it would be able to do. Turing's computer, unlike Babbage's Analytical Engine, was an abstract concept, not something he literally intended to build. He did, however, describe its workings. Passing through it would be an infinitely long tape divided into segments, each segment either marked with a slash or left blank. The machine would be able to perform only four operations: Print a new slash, erase an old one, move the tape one square to the left, or move the tape one square to the right. Turing showed that such a device, operating according to explicit instructions expressed in binary code, would be a universal computer, capable of doing anything any other computer could do.

To mathematicians, this was a startling concept: It meant that, properly constructed and programmed, any one computer could in principle do the work of all computers. This in turn suggested that a computer could be built that could do *anything* for which an algorithm—a precise and unambiguous set of instructions— could be written. This latter proposition, known as Church's thesis (after Alonzo Church, a logician Turing worked with at Princeton), is one of the cornerstones of computer science. It is also the theoretical basis for artificial intelligence.

At the time, of course, no such computer existed. A few years after his paper was published, however, Turing was installed at Bletchley Park, a rambling Victorian country house in Buckinghamshire, and put to work designing one. His employer was the British government, and the undertaking he had joined was a top-secret intelligence operation known as "Project Ultra"—a desperate effort to build a machine that could break the Nazi codes. The Poles had managed to capture one of Germany's automatic-encryption machines, a mysterious typewriter-like device known as Enigma, which was smuggled into England and set up at Bletchley. Turing was part of a topflight team of mathematicians, physicists, and electronics experts who'd been assembled there with orders to build a computer that could crack it. By the end of 1943 they'd thrown together a machine they called Colossus which did just that. It was the world's first electronic computer, and it and its prototypes were the secret weapon that kept Britain from being overrun.

Other projects were under way in America. IBM was backing one at Harvard under the direction of a navy engineer named Howard Aiken. Called the Harvard Mark I, it was completed in 1943 and with its polished steel-and-glass exterior looked very much the computer of tomorrow. Inside, however, it was the computer of yesterday, for it worked on telephone relay switches rather than the much faster (but less reliable) electronic vacuum tube. Relay switches were little gates that weighed about a gram each and actually opened and closed according to their binary state. Vacuum tubes, on the other hand, are light-bulb-like affairs that store information in the form of an electrical charge—that is, according to the absence or presence of electrons, which are so microscopic as to be all but free of inertia. It was the action of millions of individual relay gates that gave the Mark I a sound one observer compared to "a roomful of old ladies knitting away with steel needles."

The year the Harvard Mark I was finished, work began at the University of Pennsylvania on a top-secret War Department program to develop another computer—one that could calculate shell trajectories. The problem with shell trajectories was that it took too long to work them out, and a new artillery piece couldn't be put into the field until a firing table had been computed for it. That meant a delay of thirty days with the most advanced calculating machinery then available, or something like two years by conventional methods. Herman Goldstine, a mathematician at the army's Aberdeen Proving Ground in Maryland, got the Army Ordnance Corps to back two young researchers at Penn's Moore School of Engineering, John Mauchly and J. Presper Eckert, in their scheme to build a vacuum-tube computer. The war was over by the time they finished, but the machine they built was almost inconceivably fast—20,000 multiplications a minute (as opposed to ten on the Harvard Mark I). The construction of this machine —the Electronic Numerical Integrator and Calculator, or ENIAC —is generally taken as the advent of the computer age.

The next step was EDVAC, the Electronic Discrete Variable Calculator, which along with its British cousin EDSAC was the first stored-program computer—meaning it carried its instructions inside instead of having to be laboriously reprogrammed for each different task. The idea of the stored-program computer is usually attributed to John von Neumann, a Hungarian-American mathematician who'd joined the ENIAC project after a chance meeting with Goldstine at the Aberdeen train station. It was a fundamental jump, for it meant the computer could be directed to switch programs itself instead of relying on human operators to pull switches and set dials by hand. It also suggested that, imbued with sufficient intelligence, the computer might someday be able to dispense not just with human operators but with human programmers as well.

The next jump was the transistor, a device that had been invented at Bell Labs in 1948 by a three-man team headed by William Shockley. As a replacement for the vacuum tube, the transistor was unbeatable. The tube was faster than the electromechanical relay switches that had been used in the Harvard Mark I, but it still had a lot of drawbacks. Tubes took up a lot of room, they sucked up enormous quantities of power, they generated incredible amounts of heat, and they tended to burn out with alarming frequency. The transistor, like the tube, was an electronic switching device, but it was also solid-state—meaning the electrons flowed not through a glass-enclosed vacuum but through a tiny slab of solid material. The best materials were semiconductors, so-called because they conduct electricity better than insulators (wood, glass) but not as well as conductors (metal). The best semiconductor turned out to be silicon, the second most abundant element on earth.

It was the mid-fifties before transistors began to show up in computers—partly because in their early stages they were expensive and unreliable and difficult to manufacture, partly because of human inertia. But when they finally were accepted, they changed everything, because suddenly the computers could be made smaller and cheaper and much more powerful. Computers got even smaller in the early Sixties with the advent of the integrated circuit, or microchip. This device, invented in 1959, was a tiny silicon chip that contained not just a single transistor but dozens of transistors, resistors, and other circuit components.

The success of the microchip spurred efforts to achieve even greater miniaturization, and in 1971 a California chip maker known as Intel announced the development of the microprocessor—a speck of silicon containing the central processing circuitry of an entire computer. This "computer-on-a-chip" is what led to personal computers, automated tellers, pocket calculators, electronic video games, and the dozens of other new developments that have brought the computer into the realm of daily life. By the late Seventies, the refinement of the microprocessor and other LSI technologies (LSI stands for large-scale integration, the cramming of thousands of electronic components onto a single silicon chip) had reduced the computer from the size of a house to the size of a small typewriter. Intel founder Robert Noyce, writing in *Scientific American*, compared a $300 personal computer to the mighty ENIAC: The home computer "is twenty times faster, has a larger memory, consumes the power of a light bulb rather than that of a locomotive, occupies 1/30,000 the volume, and costs 1/10,000 as much."

As the computer itself shrank, the computer industry only kept expanding. California's Silicon Valley, which was full of orchards when William Shockley set up the first semiconductor company there in 1955, grew into a futuristic metropolis of computer and computer-chip manufacturers, software and video-game outfits, laser and gene-splicing firms, and science and technology think tanks, all linked together by swooping freeways and surrounded by a sea of $250,000 tract homes: the international center of high technology. Something similar developed along Route 128 around Boston, where the proximity of MIT encouraged the growth of companies like Digital Equipment and Data General. From Silicon Valley and Route 128, the industry spread even farther—to North Carolina and Arizona, to Hong Kong and Singapore, to Colorado and Ireland.

None of this, it is worth pointing out, could have happened without the stimulus of the military. From the days of ENIAC on, American computer research has depended on the Defense Department—not just for direct funding of research and development, although this has been considerable, but also as a market for innovative products. And just as World War II spurred the development of the computer itself, the cold war and the space race and the Vietnam War hastened the drive toward miniaturization.

In the early Fifties, it was the DoD that supported transistors by buying them for the guidance systems of its rockets and missiles. After *Sputnik,* the American disadvantage in booster rockets and the consequent demand for miniaturization turned the DoD and NASA into eager consumers of the first integrated circuits. Microchips went into the nose cones of nuclear warheads and the guidance systems of Vietnam-era "smart bombs"; they also made possible the high-speed "supercomputers," capable of performing hundreds of millions of operations per second, that are used to break codes, design nuclear weapons, and forecast the weather. Neither the private sector nor any other side of government has been so eager to support innovation in electronics. The computerization of society, then, has essentially been a side effect of the computerization of war.

Like many of the computers Berkeley purchased with its ARPA money, Kim is a VAX 11/780, designed and built by the Digital Equipment Corporation of Maynard, Massachusetts. What IBM is to the massive mainframe computers of science fiction and corporate bureaucracy, DEC is to the minicomputers of academic research.

The company was founded in 1957 by an MIT engineer—a circuit designer from Lincoln Labs—who had the idea that if you built computers that were small and fast and fun to run, people might prefer them to giant IBM machines that had to be tended by cults of intercedents. Three years later DEC released its first machine—the PDP-1, for Programmed Data Processor.

The PDP-1 was the first computer with a face—that is, a cathode-ray screen for displaying information and a keyboard for receiving it. Until then, computers had taken data on punch cards and processed it in batches while people sat around and waited for the results. These old "batch-processing" machines had the air of oracles, inaccessible artifacts whose workings were shrouded in mystery. The PDP-1 was different: It was a machine you could communicate with directly.

The PDP-1 was ahead of its time, but in 1965 DEC came up with the PDP-8, the machine that touched off the minicomputer revolution. Miniskirts were the rage in fashion then, and someone —it's not clear who—decided that DEC's new computer was the same thing in a machine. And the PDP-8 was not only sexy, it was cheap: It sold for $18,000 at a time when IBM's larger, slower mainframe computers cost more than a million. At that price you could buy a whole bunch of them and lash them together to form a "distributed-processing" network for racier performance. So while staider customers continued to rely on IBM for its handholding approach to programming and service, more adventuresome, sophisticated users—research labs chief among them—preferred DEC's computers, which were quick and ready and unburdened by costly support. The dominance of the mainframe was ended; this was a go-go computer for a go-go age.

Kim's immediate predecessor was the PDP-11, a more powerful version of the PDP-8. Introduced in 1969, it was destined to become the most popular minicomputer ever built. The VAX 11/780 was unveiled eight years later as a "supermini," a machine with the power of a mainframe at the price of a minicomputer. Its secret was its ability to process data in "words" of 32 bits—binary digits, zeros and ones—each.

Earlier minis had organized data into words of twelve or sixteen bits; this new 32-bit machine was both faster and endowed with far more "virtual address space." In a computer, each piece of data must be stored under its own unique "address," or binary symb ıl—and while a 16-bit computer is mathematically capable of generating a little more than 64,000 unique symbols, a 32-bit model can come up with 4,300,000,000. In computer jargon, that meant the VAX 11/780, which sold for as little as $130,000, had an astounding 4.3 gigabytes of virtual address space. Naturally, everybody wanted one.

The advent of the 32-bit supermini set off a panic among DEC's competitors—chief among them the Data General Corporation, a scrappy outfit from nearby Westborough. Data General had been founded in 1968 by a DEC engineer who'd become disgruntled, so the story goes, when some of his designs were rejected as overambitious. Organizationally, Data General is the exact antithesis of DEC: tough, mercenary, pugnacious, not at all like the humanistic concern *Fortune* once referred to as "the Gentleman Jim of minicomputers." But Data General didn't unveil its entry, the Eclipse MV/8000, until two years after DEC started making deliveries on the VAX. (The development of this machine, code-named Eagle, was the subject of Tracy Kidder's *The Soul of a New Machine*.) And as it happens, most university scientists are mild-mannered people who find it much easier to deal with DEC's fully salaried sales force than with Data General's commission-hungry pitchmen. This, plus DEC's two-year head start, helped make VAX the standard minicomputer in American research labs.

While academic researchers were delighted with the VAX 11/780, they were somewhat less enchanted with VMS, the operating system DEC had designed to run it. The operating system of a computer is the software that makes everything work together—the printer, the disk drives, the central processing unit, the applications programs that allow the computer to function as a word processor or a number cruncher or whatever. It's a control program inside the computer whose job is to send information to its proper place—to the CPU for processing or the printer for printing or an empty spot on the disk for storage. DEC has something of a reputation among computer freaks for crufty software —*crufty* being hacker slang for poorly built, overly complex— and VMS is regarded by many as just another example.

UNIX, on the other hand, has a religious following among campus hackers. Developed in the late Sixties by Berkeley's Ken

Thompson at Bell Labs, it has been licensed by AT&T to universities for so long that a whole generation of computer science students has grown up with it. Programmers who talk about it tend to use words like *lovable* and *accommodating*. Several years ago, at a meeting of ARPA-funded researchers in Washington, an intense debate broke out over the relative merits of the two systems, at the end of which it was finally decided to go with UNIX for academic research. Bill Joy, a Berkeley grad student who's regarded as the wizard of UNIX for the work he's done in modifying the system for users outside AT&T, refers to the outcome as "software Darwinism": UNIX was the system that was able to adapt and survive.

The combined popularity of the VAX minicomputer and the UNIX operating system means that for the first time since the early Sixties, when IBM mainframes were the standard, almost everyone in the academic community is using the same basic tools. This puts Kim where the action is, research-wise. Of course, that situation won't last forever. While AI researchers develop programs for the current generation of computers, the shrinking continues in microelectronics labs on both sides of the Pacific. The next stage of computer technology—the so-called fourth generation—is based on the VLSI chip. VLSI stands for "very large-scale integration," referring to integrated circuits that contain as many as 250,000 different circuit elements. This means working in dimensions of a micron—a millionth of a meter—or less, and has led to circuit designs of such complexity that humans can no longer deal with them. Computers, fortunately, are able to take over.

Now researchers have begun thinking of ways to pack as many as a billion elements onto a single chip, and the Japanese have begun their highly ambitious attempt to construct a "fifth generation" computer of such advanced design that the capacity for intelligence will be built in. The success of the fifth generation project—a ten-year, $500-million research effort coordinated by MITI, the Japanese Ministry of International Trade and Industry—will depend on radical breakthroughs in a number of areas, including VLSI and computer architecture. Among other things, the scientists of the fifth generation program are expected to abandon the serial processing design that has been the standard since the first stored-program computer was designed in the Forties. "Von Neumann machines," as the current models are called, execute their instructions one step at a time; the parallel architectures now under development will execute several steps simultaneously, thus shortening computation time dramatically.

The goal of the fifth generation project, however, is not just to produce computers that run faster—the Japanese have another project for that. The goal is to produce computers that talk, see, listen, understand, and—in some sense, at least—reason. If Japan does this first, some say, America will be in serious trouble. This is a view that was urgently expressed by Stanford's Edward Feigenbaum and science writer Pamela McCorduck in their book *The Fifth Generation*. At issue, Feigenbaum and McCorduck suggest, is nothing less than economic, cultural, and military dominance of the twenty-first century. Is America up to the challenge? "If not," they declare, "we may consign our nation to the role of the first great postindustrial agrarian society."

But the ambitions of the Japanese Institute for New Generation Computer Technology—ICOT, it's called for short—seemed a remote threat to most academic researchers on the American side of the Pacific in that spring of 1982. American business may have seemed asleep to the possibilities of artifical intelligence, but American science was not. While the scientists of ICOT were moving into their downtown Tokyo towers, their American counterparts were already deeply enmeshed in the theoretical problems of their field. There would be hardware advances to come, but the intelligent programs of the future had to be written on the computers of today. Kim No-VAX would someday face obsolescence, just like the human who inspired its name. But four years after Wilensky arrived at Berkeley, that hadn't happened yet.

3

The Riddle

Four years after he arrived at Berkeley, Wilensky had himself well set up. Kim was downstairs, ready for instruction. His research team, while still small, was nicely funded and growing rapidly: At the moment there were six Ph.D. candidates doing research and two undergraduates (Margaret Butler among them) employed as programmers. His first book was under contract: To be called *Planning and Understanding,* it would set out the theory behind the work he'd started at Yale and was continuing here. The ARPA money meant that computer science would be on a par with other disciplines at Berkeley. And the Alfred P. Sloan Foundation had just seen fit to give him $2.5 million over the next five years, which was why his picture was on the front page of the weekly newsletter of the College of Engineering.

The Sloan Foundation grant was not for artificial intelligence but for a related endeavor known as "cognitive science." Cognitive science is the study of the mind. It's an interdisciplinary approach, an attempt to link research in six different fields— anthropology, linguistics, philosophy, psychology, neuroscience, and computer science— to discover what the mind is and how it works. The mind is a riddle, and cognitive science is the mind exploring itself.

Science is the quest for knowledge. Most of science has been directed outward—at the stars, at the earth, at matter, at life.

Cognitive science is directed inward. It seeks not knowledge but metaknowledge—knowledge about knowledge itself. It requires the mind to examine the mind, to turn in on itself. Such self-referential behavior can produce strange effects. As you think about yourself remembering a fact, for example, you step up into the realm of metaknowledge; as you think about yourself thinking about yourself remembering a fact, you reach the level of metametaknowledge. This kind of stuff could go on forever—and it will if you let it, for self-reference is not unrelated to infinity. It can lead to paradox as well: Consider the self-referential remark "This sentence is false." As Douglas Hofstadter has pointed out, such paradoxes occur because any entity has a special relationship with itself, a relationship that keeps it from acting on itself the way it acts on everything else. A foot cannot step on itself, an eye cannot see itself, and a mind—will a mind be able to understand itself?

The Sloan Foundation is betting $20 million that it can, and that should count for something. The Sloan Foundation is the less splashy of New York's two great automobile philanthropies. Unlike the Ford Foundation, it doesn't conduct its business in a plate-glass cube on East Forty-second Street. Its headquarters are in a very private office suite, thickly carpeted and painted a safe beige, high above Fifth Avenue in Rockefeller Center. Nor is it in the habit of supporting causes that might be considered questionable or avant-garde. Throughout its fifty years of existence, Sloan has supported American college education in the most practical of fields—business, economics, science, engineering.

Its interest in cognition began in 1970 with the decision to support the emerging discipline of neuroscience—the study of the brain. Seven years and $15 million later, with neuroscience established as a respected academic endeavor, the officers of the foundation began looking around for something else to support. The neuroscientists suggested cognitive science. In 1976 the foundation announced that it was following their advice, and the race for funding was on.

Sloan began by inviting professors at dozens of different schools to apply for funding for a series of informal workshops. So many responded that this phase of the program came to be known as "Sloaning around." Two years later the foundation decided to fund a limited amount of research at fifteen to twenty of the most promising institutions. After that would come the crucial third phase—the one in which two or three major research centers would be named.

But at a gloves-off meeting in New Orleans in 1981, the academics convinced the foundation officers that it would be unwise to fund only a couple of schools while leaving everyone else with nothing. As a result, the money was spread out among nine different schools. Four of them got $2 million to split evenly. Stanford, Carnegie-Mellon, and the University of Pennsylvania got $1 million each. Berkeley and MIT, with $5 million between them, became the two major centers.

Berkeley's success with Sloan suggested that early estimations of Wilensky's money-seeking capabilities were not far off. With federal funding in decline and state support being cut back daily, money from corporate and foundation sources was becoming more and more important—and with individual research grants of $50,000 to $100,000 being eagerly sought, $2.5 million was the jackpot at Vegas.

Sloan wanted one major center in the East and another in the West. MIT was an obvious choice for the East: It's the home of Noam Chomsky, whose linguistic theories have inspired the dominant view of cognition. At MIT, the "Chomskyan paradigm"—the notion that language is at the core of thought, and that formal syntax, or structure, is at the core of language—is the rock upon which cognitive science is built. But at Berkeley an alternative view has developed, and this was what Wilensky stressed in his proposal.

"If you're at MIT," Wilensky explained, "the world gets more and more confused until you get to Berkeley, and then it's *crazy.*" Berkeley is strong in anthropology and cognitive psychology as well as linguistics, and in these fields it's known as a haven for intellectual unorthodoxies—particularly the position, heretical from the Chomskyan standpoint, that language should be considered in relation to factors like social structure rather than in isolation. Wilensky's computational approach to cognition is equally anti-Chomskyan in its bias and is innovative as well. (As one Sloan official remarked, "The common sense planning that Wilensky's working on—I don't think that has any parallel in cognitive psychology.") In philosophy too, Berkeley harbors the leading critics of mainstream cognitive science. If Sloan wanted to hedge its bets, then, Berkeley would be the place to do it.

As the Sloan Foundation's principal investigator at Berkeley, Wilensky's official task was to encourage the couple of dozen key faculty members in their various fields to communicate with one another. His real job, however, was to keep them from one another's throats. For at Berkeley, cognitive science consists not just of six different disciplines but of a dozen or so warring intellectual camps as well. There are mainstream cognitive psychologists and idiosyncratic anthropologists and heretical linguists. There are formalists—people who believe in the idea of a "formal" model of the mind—and there are antiformalists. And there are the two troublesome philosophers, John Searle and Hubert Dreyfus, who come from opposing philosophical traditions but who both take issue with artificial intelligence—and with cognitive science as well.

Wilensky performed his task with aplomb, presiding over weekly colloquiums and informal Friday afternoon luncheons just long enough to introduce the combatants and then stepping nimbly out of the fray. The luncheons were held in a private dining room of the Golden Bear, a campus restaurant whose costly and much-delayed renovation was threatening to bring down the student government. The colloquiums were held in the library of the Institute for Human Learning, a little room in one of the tarpaper shacks under the shadow of Evans Hall—the dark green "temporary building" known as T-4. Topics that spring included recent findings about the right and left hemispheres of the brain, sociocultural norms and their impact on language use, and a formal theory of language that was illustrated with sentences like "John saw Mary wink" and "John saw Mary wink and Bill blink." This last was particularly controversial. All formal theories are controversial at Berkeley.

The combined influence of Sloan and Schank—that is, of cognitive science and cognitive modeling—means that in AI at Berkeley, mind and computer are inextricably linked. The presence of Searle and Dreyfus lends the whole enterprise an intellectual and philosophical edge, for everything that's being done is liable to attack. But the battle lines aren't firmly drawn. To open up the question of mind and how it works is to send all sorts of demons flying out.

"AI is kind of a funny thing," Wilensky confessed one afternoon as we sat in his office on the fifth floor of Evans. It was late in the afternoon. He was through with classes for the day—his class load isn't too heavy; that would interfere with research. He was logged into Kim, writing his book on one of the two computer terminals on the table beside his desk.

Next to the door was a large poster: a NASA photograph of an attractive blue-and-white planet—Earth—surrounded by empty space. Across the bottom in large white letters was the legend LOVE YOUR MOTHER. The single window looked east, past the Beaux Arts grandeur of the Hearst Mining Building to the Berkeley Hills a few hundred yards away. It's a view of some significance: Mining is what made California, and the Hearst mining fortune is what built Berkeley.

Wilensky was trying to explain his position in the intellectual anarchy that is Berkeley today.

"From the Berkeley position, I'm very much a formalist," he was saying, "because I believe you can have all these formal theories—just not Chomsky's formal theories. But within the AI world, I'm considered somebody who's not a very formal person —not that formal at all."

How, I wanted to know, can you be formal and not formal at the same time?

"One distinction you might make is between formal theories and theories of form," Wilensky replied. "Unfortunately, formal theories usually *are* theories of form." He gave a little smile.

"What you do if you're a formal grammarian à la Chomsky is you say, 'English is a formal system, and what I'm mostly interested in is the syntactic structure of English—the *form* of English.' One issue in AI and linguistics is the issue of how important is this notion of the form of a language, the syntax of a language. Chomsky takes the extreme position that it's very important— that you can look at language as this formal symbol system and you can ask what the acceptable sets of strings are in this system, and you can do this without worrying about how you use language or that language is a medium of communication.

"There's a part of the AI world that does language which says, 'This is what we're gonna build our programs around.' But the school that I'm associated with—well, some people quote Schank as saying, 'There's no such thing as syntax.' That's probably because he said it. But it's not really what he meant. What he meant was that that's not really what's important—that it's wrong to focus on this one tiny little thing that's so little of what language is about.

"I think there's something right about that idea. Let's start worrying about the big picture." He grinned. "And when you worry about the big picture, I would like to do that by having a formal theory of what it's like."

As a Schankian, of course, Wilensky was by definition an anti-Chomskyan. Schank has been fighting Chomskyans since he was an undergraduate at Carnegie-Mellon. He went there to study math, developed an interest in linguistics, and headed for the University of Texas to pursue it further after graduation. There was a problem, however: He was interested in the psychology of language, and the linguists were only interested in structure. He couldn't believe it. He thought they were crazy. They thought the same of him.

After a couple of years, he left Texas and went back home to Brooklyn, to Bensonhurst, a Jewish neighborhood not far from where Wilensky was going to high school in Sheepshead Bay. He sat there for a month and thought. It was 1968, and he'd heard there were computer jobs in California. He drove to San Francisco, moved into a hippie crash pad, and landed a job at Stanford as a researcher in a computerized psychiatry project. His boss was Kenneth Colby, a proponent of computerized therapy who's known for two legendary programs: DOCTOR, a psychiatrist program that mimics the responses of a Rogerian therapist; and PARRY, a paranoid program so convincing that a panel of experts was unable to distinguish it from a paranoid human.

A year after he arrived, Schank got a Ph.D. from Texas through the mail and joined the Stanford linguistics faculty. He was twenty-three. He did his research at the AI lab, but he ran into the same problem there that he was always encountering in linguistics: too many formalists. At the AI lab they were mathematical formalists, people determined to build predicate calculus models of the brain. Schank was interested in building cognitive models—programs that worked according to the principles of psychology rather than formal logic. He felt that language was the key to intelligence; they thought language and intelligence didn't have much to do with each other. In 1974 he left for Yale, where there was no AI and no one to tell him what it should be.

The cognitive approach is what distinguishes Schank and his students from others in the field. What is the mind? How does it work? Philosophers have been mulling these questions since the time of Plato. Psychologists have been searching for a scientific explanation for a century, and neuroscientists have just started working at the biological level. AI researchers of the cognitive school have added another dimension to the question: Can the workings of the mind be duplicated on a computer?

During the eighteenth century, the mind—like everything else, it seems—was commonly likened to a clock. Now the vogue is to compare it to an information-processing system—a computer. The mind receives input, and the mind produces output. The mind processes the data our sensory organs provide and creates the series of neural impulses we call "reality." Bishop Berkeley argued that reality consists only of our perceptions. *"Esse est percipi,"* he declared—"to be is to be perceived." The information-processing model would amend this dogma: In the last quarter of the twentieth century, to be is to be processed.

But how does that processing occur? That's what cognitive scientists want to know. They view the mind as a system that manipulates symbols, and they seek to model the algorithms—the precise and unambiguous set of instructions—that seem to guide it. That these algorithms exist is taken for granted.

"Possibly the basic notion in cognitive science," Wilensky declared, leaning back in his chair as the shadows grew long across the hills, "is the notion that the mind represents things, and that what we have to do is represent how the mind represents stuff. So what we do in our computer programs and our formal theories is to say, 'How is it that all this stuff is coded away in the mind?' And what we need to do is devise notations for describing this sort of thing."

So Wilensky views AI as the key to the mind, and he views the mind as the key to AI—to the creation of intelligent machines.

When I asked him which he was more committed to, mind or machine, he smiled slyly and said, "My loyalties are divided."

AI at Berkeley means natural-language processing and common sense reasoning. Of all the subdomains in the world of artificial intelligence, natural language and common sense are the most unlikely.

To date, the area in which researchers have been most successful—successful in terms of getting results, and of attracting money and attention and excitement because they've produced something that actually works—has been expert systems. Research in computer vision and robotics, though still in the early stages, has progressed to the point that rudimentary systems are available to industrial customers. Efforts in automated problem-solving, automated theorem-proving, and automated chess-playing—three areas that first attracted AI researchers in the Fifties—have been even more successful. All they've really demonstrated, however, is that playing decent chess or solving mathematical puzzles may not be such an intelligent activity after all.

AI, as many observers have noted, is a field of constantly receding horizons: As soon as one realm has been conquered, a whole new vista opens up. In this case, it turns out that solving the cannibals-and-missionaries problem (how can three missionaries cross the river with three cannibals in a two-man canoe when the missionaries will be eaten if they're ever outnumbered?) or proving theorems from Bertrand Russell's *Principia Mathematica* isn't really that impressive. A computer can do these things, just as a computer can perform arithmetic calculations at inhuman speed—but is that any demonstration of intelligence?

The classic test of machine intelligence was proposed by Alan Turing in 1950, in a paper called "Computing Machinery and Intelligence." Turing's idea, expressed years before any serious work on artificial intelligence had begun, was that in order for a computer to be deemed intelligent, it must pass as a human in a blind test. This "Turing test," as it's come to be known, would be set up so the judge could communicate through a teletype machine with a human and a machine. He could talk to them about anything he liked, and at the end he would have to decide which was which. Both the computer and the human would be free to give false answers, so it wouldn't do any good to ask one of them how good a driver he was, for example, or when he last saw his mother.

In his paper, Turing predicted that a machine would pass his test before the end of the century. But he himself would not live to see it, for in 1954, at the age of forty-one, he retreated to his home laboratory and bit into an apple that had been dipped in cyanide. His mother maintained it was an accident; his friends had a different explanation. Two years earlier he had revealed himself to the authorities as a homosexual, and the result had been a forced regimen of hormone treatments that amounted to chemical castration. Turing's "accident," it seems, was a cleverly disguised imitation.

Now, thirty years later, Turing's successors seem very little closer to producing a machine that can pass his "imitation game" than they were at the time of his death. The reason is the unforeseen difficulty they've encountered with natural language and common sense reasoning—particularly the latter. The early concentration on getting computers to perform sophisticated tasks—playing expert chess, solving complex puzzles, proving mathematical theorems—proved only that it was possible to do these things and still be incredibly stupid about the world. It showed that what's important about human intelligence is not our highly developed powers of logic but ordinary, old-fashioned common sense—horse sense, if you will. It was an unexpected yet oddly reassuring discovery.

Something similar has happened in vision and robotics. As research progressed, it became apparent that the truly hard things for machines are what's easiest for humans. The biggest problem with robots, for example, is "obstacle avoidance"—not bumping into things. Vision systems have a lot of trouble with "edge detection"—figuring out where one thing begins and another one ends. For the programmer, the difficulty lies in figuring out how a computer should process the extraordinary detail a typical image contains. Humans seem to have some sort of automatic filtering mechanism that tells us what's important and what isn't. Computers simply get lost in an overwhelming mass of information. In a very literal sense, they can't see the forest for the trees.

All these problems have a couple of factors in common. One is that while it's relatively easy to program computers with skills that humans have to learn, it's very difficult to program them with the skills we acquire unconsciously. This shouldn't be too surprising, for no one has access to the unconscious mind. It functions automatically, at a level we are only beginning to understand. The physical processes that enable us to see, to remember, to carry on a conversation, to function in the everyday world—all these remain a mystery.

The other difficulty is that in order for a machine to function in an unrestricted environment—that is, the real world—it needs to have a complex model of what the world is like. In order to play chess, a computer doesn't need to know about anything but chess. But to carry on an intelligent conversation in English about, say, fishing, it needs to know about fish, people, sport, water, weather, worms, and getting up at five in the morning, not to mention the difference between a riverbank and a savings bank and what any given pronoun is supposed to refer to. In other words, it needs to have a vast array of knowledge about the world, and it needs to have it organized in such a way that it can be accessed instantly on demand. Little wonder, then, that a writer in *Scientific American* has concluded that dealing with ordinary language and simulating common sense were two of the greatest challenges facing AI researchers today—or that John McCarthy once predicted it would be 300 years before computers were as adept as people at exhibiting common sense.

So Wilensky and his team have been tackling the most difficult and unlikely branch of a difficult and unlikely field. They're trying to find a way of representing basic human knowledge—knowledge about language, knowledge about the world—so efficiently that even Kim No-VAX will be able to understand it. That means discovering the essence of what is human, and translating it into the precise and formal renderings of computer code.

Of course, that's not how they talk about it. They talk about knowledge representation and data structures and frame invocation. But it means the same thing. It means they're trying to give knowledge to a computer named Kim. It means they're engaged in an undertaking as Promethean as the toils of Mary Shelley's

Frankenstein—or possibly as ridiculous as those of Mel Brooks's counterpart.

Their work is based on Schank's ideas, and on the theories Wilensky began developing at Yale. These are theories of goal interaction—how plans and goals come into play in everyday human life. They're an outgrowth of the work Wilensky did for his doctorate.

Schank was just setting up his AI effort at the time, and while most of his students were working on his main story-understander program, SAM, Wilensky was put to work on a more speculative cousin known as PAM, for "Plan-Applier Mechanism." Where SAM was supposed to understand stories because it knew about scripts, PAM was envisioned as a program that could understand stories about situations for which no ready-made script exists. PAM would know about plans and goals. These, Schank theorized, are what enable people to function in situations they've never encountered before.

Ten years ago, nobody in artificial intelligence had really thought to tackle the problem Wilensky was given—to build a story understander that knew about plans. Most of the planning work that had been done in AI was in the area of "robot planning" —programming robots to move blocks around. At Carnegie-Mellon, Newell and Simon had been concerned with human problem-solving, which is one aspect of planning, but they dealt with elaborate puzzles and mathematical games, not with the mundane details of day-to-day existence. In the conventional thinking of the AI community, such concerns were hardly deemed worthy of consideration.

And so PAM was unique. It was given detailed knowledge about plans and goals—what they are, how they arise, how they interact with each other. This enabled it to figure out motivations —why somebody would want to do something. Told that John had proposed to Mary, for example, it would infer that he had the goal of marrying her and that his proposal was part of a plan for achieving that goal.

At the 1980 meeting of the American Association for the Advancement of Science, Wilensky demonstrated PAM's expertise with the following story:

John needed some money so he got a gun and went to a liquor store and he told the owner he wanted some money and the owner gave John the money and John left.

and the following question:

Q: Why did the owner give John the money?
A: The owner was afraid John would hurt him.

As a report in MIT's *Technology Review* observed, PAM clearly knew more than it had been told.

By that time, Wilensky had started setting up his own research team at Berkeley. In the next two years, as the Berkeley AI team grew, people started working on a whole series of programs. Each program was designed to use a shared store of knowledge, and each program modeled different facets of basic human intelligence: planning, understanding, language.

There were two language programs, PHRED and PHRAN. PHRAN was supposed to understand natural language, PHRED to produce it—or rather, technically speaking, PHRAN was designed to "process" natural language, PHRED to "generate" it. PHRAN, which stands for PHRasal ANalyser, was built by Yigal Arens. It translates English sentences into internal "meaning representations" which the computer can deal with. PHRED, which stands for PHRasal English Diction, had been started by a master's candidate and taken over by a new student from Harvard, Paul Jacobs. It works the other way, translating the meaning representations into English.

Marc Luria, a philosophy major from Columbia, was working on a program that answers questions in conceptual-dependency form. Unlike the other programs, Luria's had no name. There's a tradition in AI of calling programs by jazzy acronyms—SAM for Script-Applier Mechanism, STRIPS for STanford Research Institute Problem-Solver. The vision group at Stanford actually has a program named ACRONYM that doesn't stand for anything. Luria, however, was just getting started. He wasn't ready for that yet.

The other two programs were called PAMELA and PANDORA. PAMELA, which had started out as an extension of PAM, was being written by Peter Norvig, a tall, blond New Englander who'd come to Berkeley from Brown. It was intended to give PAM a greater depth of understanding, enabling it not just to figure out why John would propose to Mary (because he wanted to marry her—not such a great answer when you think about it), but also to associate that proposal with things like wedding rings and love.

Joe Faletti was writing PANDORA, a problem-solving program whose expertise was in the area of common sense planning. There were already computer programs to solve every imaginable type of problem—algebraic problems, structural design problems, nuclear-engineering problems, nuclear-explosion problems, figuring-out-your-income-tax problems. Faletti had decided on a different approach from all these. He was designing a computer program that would solve the ordinary problems of everyday human existence.

In the spring of 1982, Faletti was trying to get PANDORA to come up with a plan for picking up a newspaper in the rain. PANDORA had been programmed to believe it was a person who'd just awakened and who wanted to know what was going on in the world. She knows there's a newspaper on the front lawn, and she notices that it's raining outside, and she knows she wants to stay dry, so she needs to come up with a plan for getting the paper without getting wet. Faletti's idea was that she should put on a raincoat.

For a human, this is pretty trivial stuff. For a computer, it's not. Fetching an object in the rain requires a lot of knowledge— knowledge about rain and raincoats, outdoors and indoors, being dry and being wet. Humans learn these things gradually, as babies. Computers come into the world full-grown and ignorant. They don't even know enough to stay in out of the rain. But even though I knew all this, I couldn't deny an almost dizzying sense of absurdity when I first heard about PANDORA. I felt as if I'd entered some sort of bizarre computational netherworld where the Promethean and the quixotic had somehow merged.

"Welcome to AI," Wilensky said with a smile.

4

The PANDORA Program

Joe Faletti had not started out to teach a computer when to put on its raincoat. He had started out, some twelve years before, studying math and English as an undergraduate at Berkeley. He had come to this only by accident.

He'd grown up in Antioch, California, an industrial town on the Sacramento River, halfway between San Francisco and Sacramento. Antioch and neighboring Pittsburg are like specks of the American industrial heartland on the edge of California's vast inland delta. It's a bleak piece of country, dry grass and mountains on the edge of the flat, marshy wetlands, with empty mills on the riverfront and abandoned coal mines in the hills. Joe's father works in a steel mill; both his grandfathers did the same.

Joe is the oldest of six children, all of them boys. His mother is religious, his father a tinkerer. Joe takes after his father. He likes to pull things apart; he likes to know how things work. He has an engineer's curiosity and a humanist's breadth of interest. That's how he ended up in AI.

"It's really a neat field," he said, wiping a shock of coal-black hair off his forehead. "It's the kind of field you can go home and talk about. When you start thinking about these things and you're with your family, all of a sudden you just stop and say, 'Now how did I do that?' Which can be really disconcerting for your family."

Joe went into computer science as a grad student. The first five years he spent exploring various avenues of study, AI among them. He took an introductory course from Lotfi Zadeh—this was before Wilensky arrived—and after that a course in computational linguistics, which involves using computers to study language. In the computational-linguistics course he met some other people who'd taken Zadeh's AI course and who'd formed a study group to learn more. They called themselves the Frames Group, after a theory Marvin Minsky had come up with in 1974.

One of the chief problems—maybe *the* chief problem—in artificial intelligence is the one known as knowledge representation: how to represent facts in a computer program so they can be accessed on demand. In humans this happens automatically: We don't have to think about how to store what we know about love, say, or the behavior that's expected of us in restaurants; we either store it or we don't. With computers it's different: Every fact the computer needs must be written out in code, and it must be organized in such a way that the computer can integrate it with every other fact it has. Only with the ability to access its knowledge of the world—to riffle through the mind in search of the appropriate information—can any being exhibit intelligent behavior.

What Minsky did was to introduce the idea of storing knowledge in "frames." Frames are data structures full of details, details that can be added or taken out at will. It was basically a method of organization. Minsky outlined the concept in an influential paper, then left it to others to work out the implementation. In the past ten years, it has served as the basis for AI programs in every area from computer vision to natural language processing.

The Frames Group at Berkeley was essentially an informal discussion club. Its members used to get together once a week to discuss developments in AI. One person would read a paper on what somebody was doing somewhere else, and then they'd all talk about it. At times as many as a dozen people showed up, but usually it was more like six.

It was Faletti who insisted they start every meeting by watching "Mork and Mindy" for tips. At first, the others thought he was kidding. But when it came his turn to host the meeting—the meetings were held in a different apartment each Thursday night at 8:00—he told them he was going to be watching "Mork and

Mindy" and those who didn't want to should come at 8:30. Most people came at 8:00. After that, "Mork and Mindy" took up the first half-hour of each meeting.

"It was great fun," Faletti told me. "Here you had this character who knew very little about anything, and who was continually misunderstanding things because he didn't make inferences that other people were making. He had all these high-level reasoning powers but not the knowledge, and he had all these preconceptions that were just completely different from Earth people's. Spaceships on Ork were egg-shaped, so anything having to do with eggs reminded him of that. Besides that, he considered an egg to already be a living being, so at one point they had him throwing an egg up and saying 'Fly, little bird, fly!' So you could analyze the jokes he made and see what processes were failing and why."

After a while, Mork learned too much about Earth, and the AI aficionados of the Frames Group lost interest. About the time that happened, however, Wilensky arrived on campus. The members of the Frames Group were frankly suspicious. Their computational-linguistics course had been taught by a proponent of KRL—Knowledge Representation Language, an experimental AI language that puts a lot of emphasisis on placing knowledge in context. They weren't at all sure they liked Schank's ideas, especially conceptual dependency, which reduces all actions to a series of basic primitives—primitives that by nature are context-free. But Joe found Wilensky to be reasonable enough, and before long he was asking him to be his research adviser. He was one of only two members of the Frames Group to do so.

Since he'd been in graduate school for five years without ever settling on a research project, Joe was beginning to experience some bureaucratic pressure to get started. That meant he had to take his qualifying exams—oral examinations in which you show that you know what's been done in your field and you're ready to start some original research. But Joe wasn't ready to do anything in AI, so Wilensky gave him a 7,000-page reading list. When he'd worked his way through half of it, they started talking about research projects he might undertake. Joe said he'd like to do some natural-language work, but that he might like to have a little problem-solving stuff in there too.

At that point, the only research Wilensky had going was PAM and the theory of goal interaction that made it work. This included some theory about how plans and goals might be connected, but no theory about how plans are actually made. So Wilensky gave a copy of his thesis to Joe with the suggestion that he think about how PAM's operations might be applied to a planner—specifically, a planner that has goals of its own and can detect conflicts between them. Joe went off and started thinking, and for the next six weeks the two of them met weekly to discuss what he was thinking about.

Most of those discussions centered around two hypothetical situations a planning program might have to deal with. The first of these was something Joe spent a lot of time talking with his mom about. Imagine you're home cooking dinner when a friend calls. He's in town only for the evening and he wants to see you. What do you do? Put some more food on the stove? Pitch your dinner and go out to a restaurant? Invite your friend to come over later? Growing up in a family of eight, Joe had seen his mother deal with problems like this all the time. He decided he'd use it as one of the examples for his quals.

The other example was based on one of Wilensky's standard instances of goal conflict—wanting to watch a football game on TV when you have a paper due the next day. Joe's problem was that he was perfectly capable of writing a paper while watching TV, so he couldn't see any goal conflict. But what if, instead of having to write a paper, you discovered that your mother was in the hospital recovering from an emergency appendectomy? The solution, assuming your mother likes football, would be to realize that there are TV sets in hospital rooms and that you could watch football and visit your mother at the same time.

Does Joe's mother in fact like football?

"No," he admitted. "*I* don't even like football."

There was one other example that occurred to him, a complex planning situation he'd actually found himself in once. It was far too complicated to use right away, but someday he hoped to get PANDORA to function under the same circumstances.

He was home eating lunch, reading a book, and listening to the radio when suddenly the radio went dead. At first he thought the station had lost its signal, so he waited for it to come back. When it didn't, he checked the radio and then the lights and then the refrigerator and discovered the power had gone off in his apartment. The lights were on in the hallway, so he knew it wasn't the whole building—but he didn't know if the building had emergency power or not. He checked to see if he'd blown a fuse, but it wasn't that, so he headed downstairs to check the power boxes. As he went outside, he heard someone using a power saw, so he knew it wasn't a general power failure. When he got to the basement garage, he discovered that someone had run a car into the main power box, but that all the hallway lights were on a separate power box—so the only part of the building with electricity was the halls.

"Now, the key thing there," Joe explained to me, "is all the knowledge I had about where power comes from and what causes it to fail. And also, given that knowledge, how do you actually figure out what's causing the problem?"

Joe's plan for the day had been to take a shower after lunch and go to campus. When he got upstairs, he decided to go to campus without showering and hope the power would be back on when he got home. It wasn't. So he went through the evening doing all the things you do without thinking, only this time there wasn't any power. He'd turn on the light and it wouldn't come on. He'd start to open the refrigerator and think, No, the power's out. I'd better leave it closed. He got a can of chili down from the cupboard and switched on the stove, only to realize it wasn't working. At that point he decided to get a flashlight—but instead of going to the Radio Shack a block away, he walked six blocks to a grocery store.

"What that says to me," he explained, "is that my default plan for buying something I needed was to go to the grocery store. I didn't consider the fact that maybe there's a specialty store to go to for a flashlight."

I told Joe that I'd suspected all along that this was the kind of stuff people have trouble with.

Joe agreed. "Potentially we could build a home adviser-type thing. You say, 'My power's out, how do I fix dinner?'"

"That's right," I said, "a common sense computer program to solve all your goal conflicts."

"Of course," Joe added soberly, "if your power was out, you couldn't . . ."

Joe's quals committee was a five-man group headed by Zadeh, with Wilensky one of its members. They gave him the go-ahead to begin his research. He had to finish learning how to program in LISP, and then he sat down and started working on PANDORA.

The first thing he had to do was come up with a name. He knew it should probably start with a *P* because it was a planner, so he wrote out a dozen names that started with *P.* PANDORA was the one he settled on. It stood for Plan ANalyzer with Dynamic Organization, Revision, and Application—a sensible name, he thought, because his program would be designed to analyze plans for conflicts, revise them if any conflicts were detected, and apply them when they were determined to be conflict-free. Of course, fidelity to purpose wasn't his only consideration. "When you're choosing a name, you want something that's easy to remember," he admitted, a trifle ruefully. "And I was actually kind of worried about PANDORA, because it's a little long."

When he started, Joe assumed that people have a model of the future in which all their plans are laid out. He also assumed that most goal conflicts are time-based—that you might be able to do almost anything, but you couldn't do two things at once. After a while he discovered that this wasn't true of all goal conflicts, just the ones in his examples. Before he realized that, though, he learned that time is very difficult to represent in a computer program—so difficult, in fact, that most people in AI have managed to avoid it. He tried mapping out his model of the future as a time sequence with overlapping intervals, but then he had to figure out how to notice that two time intervals overlap. It was, he discovered, "a hairy computational problem."

Joe also came to realize that he had no idea how to represent all the goals associated with being a host in the friend-who-calls-at-dinnertime story. He tried cutting it down to just a planning-dinner story—noticing that you're hungry, deciding to cook dinner, and figuring out what to have and how to cook it—but even that was too complicated. So a year after taking his quals, he and Wilensky started talking about newspaper-and-raincoat stories.

That was two years ago. Joe had seized on the raincoat example as something he could get PANDORA to handle quickly so he could write a paper on it for IJCAI—the International Joint Conference on Artificial Intelligence, which was to be held a few months later in Vancouver. He didn't make it. After that he'd spent a lot of time teaching undergraduate courses in introductory programming and data structures, and he'd spent even more time working with Wilensky and Mike Deering, his friend from the Frames Group, on a new computer language called PEARL —Package for Efficient Access to Representations in LISP. PEARL is essentially an extension of LISP that's designed to speed up the data base that serves as a program's memory. In a paper that did make it into the IJCAI proceedings, PEARL's authors claimed that it made PAM an order of magnitude faster, enabling it to do what had taken 5.6 seconds of processing time in only 0.56 seconds.

Deering went on to do computer vision—he wrote his thesis on a "blind guidance device," a computer on a cart that works in tandem with a shoulder-mounted camera to warn blind people of obstacles ahead—and then took a job in the AI lab at Fairchild. Joe did a little more work on PEARL and then, with the beginning of the winter quarter, returned to PANDORA full-time. His immediate goal was to get it working in time to meet the deadline for papers for the conference that AAAI—the American Association for Artificial Intelligence—was holding that summer in Pittsburgh. His long-term goal was considerably more ambitious. "As a problem solver," he said, "PANDORA is supposed to be the controller of all conscious thought. But if PANDORA puts her raincoat on this week, I'll be a lot happier."

It was about the time Joe returned to PANDORA that the AI team started using Kim. Before then, they'd been using a much older PDP-10. Kim had the advantage of running under UNIX, which is a much friendlier operating system than the PDP-10's; but because Fateman was using it for his hardware experimentation, it had the disadvantage of being down more often than most machines. In theory they could use any machine on the computer science division's network of VAXes, since their terminals were hooked up to a "plug board" that offered access to all of them. In practice, though, they used Kim, because Kim was the one Wilensky owned a piece of.

At the same time they got Kim, the AI team moved into larger quarters—a rectangular office on the fifth floor of Evans, with a window overlooking the northern edge of campus and the Berkeley Hills beyond. Though bigger than their old office around the corner, it was still crowded with desks and chairs—all of them were normal, metal office desks and normal, vinyl-cushioned office chairs except for Joe's. Joe had an incongruously large, squeaky, old-fashioned oak office chair and a child's school desk with a wood-grained Formica top. It was, he'd discovered; the perfect height for typing.

The office had a beige vinyl-tile floor and beige wallboard walls and a beige concrete ceiling with fluorescent lights overhead. But it was hardly devoid of personality. On the door, Yigal had taped a "Dear Abby" letter from the *San Francisco Chronicle* and Joe had posted a comic strip from the science-fiction magazine *Beyond*. The "Dear Abby" letter was from a twenty-two-year-old music lover who'd come away from a Barry Manilow concert convinced that God had put her on earth to devote her life to a lonely person like Barry, or if not him then Burt Reynolds. The comic strip was called "Boid" and was more to the point. "Think yer smart, don't ya?" said a bird to a computer. "Mebbie you can compute numbahs faster than us livin' creatures . . . But can you feel? Can you laff & cry, an' hate, an' love? Na, computer, fer all yer smarts, you'll never replace us." Then the bird flew away— and the computer said, "Oh, well, I can dream, can't I?"

Kim had no such ambitions. Kim had no ambitions at all except the ones it was programmed to have. And the only ambitions it got from PANDORA were the goals written into the newspaper-and-raincoat story: Get the newspaper, and don't get wet.

Kim's presence in the office was signaled by the computer terminals, which were connected by cables to the plug board in the fourth-floor machine room. There was nothing particularly futuristic-looking about these terminals; they were two-tone console units, light blue over dark blue, with the wind-sculptured look of a 1958 Chevy. On the wall across the room, someone had tacked a map of the brain, and next to that was a large plastic whiteboard that could be written on with Magic Marker. There were also two art posters that Peter Norvig had picked up at the Harvard Coop: a Kandinsky that had caught his eye and Klee's *Viaducts,* which he'd gotten because they looked like arches. Arches are a milestone in the history of AI: One of the first learning programs, developed at MIT in 1970, was designed to learn what an arch is from examples and counterexamples.

On a chilly day in March, not long after Yigal's talk on MOPs, I found Joe at one of the terminals, running PANDORA on Kim. He was wearing brown-and-white-checked polyester pants and a matching knit shirt. Yigal was at the other terminal helping David Chin, the newest member of the AI team, with a programming problem. It was late in the afternoon.

The screen in front of Joe was covered with lists of words surrounded by parentheses. That was LISP. The computer language used by most AI programmers, LISP had been developed at MIT a quarter-century earlier by John McCarthy as a way of manipulating nonnumerical symbols—that is, words and phrases. The only other computer language still in use from that time is FORTRAN (FORmula TRANslator), which was developed to handle mathematical expressions. Most early programming was done in machine language—binary code, zeros and ones. LISP programs, which are automatically translated into machine language by a separate program called an "interpreter," consist of lists of words set off by parentheses. These parentheses form nests, and nests within nests within nests; as a program is run, it moves through the nests in a progression as logical and orderly as reason itself.

But PANDORA wasn't written in just LISP. PANDORA was written in a dialect of LISP, with PEARL added. Computer languages, like natural languages, tend to develop dialects over time. Of course, it's not the computers that develop the little mutations that set dialects apart; it's the humans who program them. AI programmers at MIT use MACLISP; at Xerox they use InterLISP; and at Berkeley they use a variant of MACLISP that carries the whimsical name (given to it by Fateman) of Franz Lisp. The particular version of Franz Lisp in use at the time was Opus 38. PANDORA, then, was written in Franz Lisp, Opus 38, plus PEARL.

In addition, of course, all of PANDORA's actions were represented as variants of Roger Schank's conceptual-dependency "primitives"—ATrans, MTrans, PTrans, and so forth. For the newspaper-and-raincoat story, only two primitives were required: PTrans, for moving outside and inside; and Grasp, for picking up the newspaper. All the nouns in the program were represented as "slot-filler objects"—that is, tiny bits of knowledge in a slot labeled "actor," for example, or "object," or "to" or "from." Anytime a slot was left blank, it would be followed by the word *nilstruct*— short for *empty structure.* PANDORA, then, was actually a sort of giant fill-in-the-blanks that could think.

Joe punched a key on the keyboard and a string of words appeared on the screen:

```
Next event:
  (Time Of Day (Time Morning))
Looking for goals for daytime:
  (Time Of Day (Time Morning))
Adding daytime goals:
  (Know (Object
        (State (Object (Object
                       (Ident World))))))
        (Knower (Person
                (Ident Ego))))
```

"Next event" told PANDORA that it was morning. "Adding daytime goals" loaded in the goal of knowing something—specifically, the state of some object whose identity is the world. It further specified that the knower was a person whose identity was "ego"—PANDORA itself. In other words, PANDORA had just been programmed to know that it was morning and that it was a person who wanted to know what was going on in the world. More strings appeared on screen:

```
Next event:
  (Weather
(Object (Location (Ident Outside)))
(Condition Raining)
1 <Enter> WatchAts
  ((Weather
(Object (Location (Ident Outside)))
(Condition Raining))
```

"Next event" told PANDORA that the weather at the location whose identity was outside was "condition raining." That triggered "WatchAts" to come in. "WatchAts," I had been warned, is something AI programmers call a "demon."

"A demon," Joe explained, "is a process that you want to be waiting in the background. It watches everything that happens, and when you get the conditions that say it's appropriate for it to run, it runs. In the newspaper-in-the-rain situation, if it's raining and you hear someone's going outside, you need to know they're going to get wet, and you need to know that automatically. You don't want to have to think, 'Okay, I'm going outside—does that mean I'm going to get wet?' What you want is something that says, 'Hey, if you go outside, you're going to get wet!' if it's raining, and otherwise leaves you alone." As he spoke, yet more lists scrolled across the screen:

```
Normal planner for:
  (Know (Object
           (State (Object
                     (Object
                        (Ident World)))))
           (Knower (Person (Ident Ego))))
Normal plan found:
  ((PTrans (Actor (Person (Ident Ego)))
          (Effects
              ((At (Object (Person (Ident Ego)))
                  (Spot (Location
                             (Ident Outside))))))
          (Object (Person (Ident Ego)))
          (To (Location (Ident Outside)))
          (From (nilstruct)))
   (Grasp (Actor (Person (Ident Ego)))
          (Effects nil)
          (Object (Object (Ident Newspaper))))
   (PTrans (Actor (Person (Ident Ego)))
          (Effects
              ((At (Object
                      (Person
                        (Ident Ego)))
                  (Spot
                     (Location
                        (Ident Inside))))))
          (Object (Person (Ident Ego)))
          (To (Location (Ident Inside)))
          (From (nilstruct))))
```

"This says that the normal plan for knowing what's going on in the world is to go outside, pick up the newspaper, and go back inside." he continued. "Now what I want to do is simulate that plan to figure out whether it's going to work or not. The way I simulate it is to assert its effects to see if they're okay. That's one way of noticing that you're going to get wet, because an effect of going outside is that you'll *be* outside, and being outside when it's raining is where the inference comes in."

By that time, PANDORA had already started asserting the effects of its actions.

```
Asserting Effects of:
   (PTrans (Actor (Person (Ident Ego)))
           (Effects
             ((At (Object (Person (Ident Ego)))
                  (Spot (Location (Ident
                        Outside))))))
           (Object (Person (Ident Ego)))
           (To (Location (Ident Outside)))
           (From (nilstruct)))
Effects is:
   (At (Object (Person (Ident Ego)))
       (Spot (Location (Ident Outside))))
```

—and that caused two more demons to kick in:

```
1 <Enter> RainCheck
   ((At (Object (Person (Ident Ego)))
        (Spot (Location (Ident Outside)))))
:1 <Enter> WatchDryness
    ((Dryness (Object (Person (Ident Ego)))
              (Degree Soaking)))
```

Joe was looking as excited as a kid in a video arcade. He was leaning forward in his chair, his face nearly touching the screen. "See, when it asserts that the effects of the first PTrans are that it's going to be outside, this demon RainCheck says, 'Hey, wait a minute! You're going to be outside, and that means I should watch for dryness!' And then WatchDryness says, 'Oops! You're going to be soaking!' That creates a goal conflict between the PTrans and wanting to be dry—so we invoke Resolve-Goal-Conflict."

I had heard about Resolve-Goal-Conflict before. In a paper called "Meta-Planning" which had been published in the journal *Cognitive Science,* Wilensky had outlined the theory that lay at the bottom of all this. The basic idea was that programs such as PAM and PANDORA—that is, story-understander programs and problem-solver programs—could have two distinct types of knowledge: knowledge about the world, and knowledge about planning. The planning knowledge, instead of being buried in the program or stuck in as needed, would be explicitly stated in a way that made it easy to get to. It would consist of "higher-level" plans and goals, or what Wilensky referred to as "meta-plans" and "meta-goals"—plans for making plans, and goals to keep in mind during the planning process. This way, Wilensky argued, both programs—the story understander and the problem solver—would be able to share their knowledge about planning.

To flesh out his theory, Wilensky devised a whole system of plans and meta-plans, goals and meta-goals, themes and meta-themes. Themes he defined as general ideas that give rise to specific goals; meta-themes as general ideas that give rise to specific meta-goals. The "Don't Violate Desirable States" theme, for example, initiates the "Preserve-Endangered-State" goal; since PANDORA recognizes dryness as a desirable state, this gives her the goal of preserving her own dryness—that is, of not getting wet. Likewise, the "Achieve As Many Goals As Possible" meta-theme initiates the "Resolve-Goal-Conflict" meta-goal. This tells PANDORA that she has the meta-goal of resolving the conflict between her original goal of going outside to pick up the newspaper and her new goal of not getting wet.

"Now," said Joe, with the authoritative air of a man who plays for hours on a single quarter, "we have this goal of resolving the goal conflict. Normal plan for that is to PutOn raincoat. So we assert the effects of putting on a raincoat, which I haven't put in, and we assert the effects of PTransing outside, and—"

I looked carefully at the screen:

```
Asserting effects of:
   (PutOn (Actor (Person (Ident Ego))))
           (Effects nil)
```

```
                (Object (Object (Ident Raincoat)))).
Effects is:
 (Nil)
Asserting effects of:
   (PTrans (Actor (Person (Ident Ego)))
           (Effects
             ((At (Object
                     (Person (Ident Ego)))
                  (Spot
                     (Location (Ident
                     Outside))))))
           (Object (Person (Ident Ego)))
           (To (Location (Ident Outside)))
           (From (nilstruct)))
Effects is:
   (At (Object (Person (Ident Ego)))
       (Spot (Location (Ident Outside))))
1 <Enter> RainCheck
   ((At (Object (Person (Ident Ego)))
       (Spot (Location (Ident Outside)))))
:1 <Enter> WatchDryness
   ((Dryness (Object (Person (Ident Ego)))
             (Degree Soaking)))
```

I was confused. Why had RainCheck come back in? What was WatchDryness doing there this time? And what was all this about Degree Soaking? Hadn't PANDORA put her raincoat on?

Joe burst out laughing. "This doesn't work because it doesn't know that because it has the raincoat on, it won't get wet. I haven't gotten that far yet. See up here? It's asserting the effects of the plan, and it says the effects of PutOn are nil and the effects of this PTrans are it's going outside, and then it runs the demon that says, 'Oh, it's raining, you're going to get wet!' So it keeps saying 'Oh! Got to put a raincoat on!'—over and over again."

I stood up and looked around. Yigal and David had finished their programming and were playing Pac-Man on Kim. A computer can do anything it's been programmed to do. Kim has the Pac-Man program on her systems software.

5

"John Loves Mary"

In computer terms, what had happened to PANDORA was that it had fallen into an infinite loop. If allowed to continue, it would have kept putting its raincoat on endlessly, never realizing that it had resolved its conflicting goals, or that it had any choice but to keep repeating the action it had been programmed to take. In fact, it didn't have any choice.

All PANDORA knew about the world was what it had been programmed to know; and in the primitive state of of its programming, a crucial piece of information had been left out: Raincoats keep you dry. This flaw left it locked in a pattern of endless repetition. It put on a raincoat because it was the normal plan for going out in the rain, but it didn't know the raincoat would keep it dry; so it put on a raincoat because it was the normal plan for going out in the rain, but it didn't know the raincoat would keep it dry; so it . . . and so on. It's a problem no human is ever likely to face.

For computers, however, it's not unusual. Twenty years ago, CBS aired a television program in which some MIT students got to show off the creative abilities of a computer known as TXO. This computer had been programmed to write television scripts, and the network had hired a couple of actors and produced one of the scripts—a western, as it happened. The result was a pretty conventional Wild West shoot-out: A bank robber returns to his hideaway cabin with a couple of bags of gold, the sheriff sneaks up on him as he's taking a shot of whiskey, and the robber is killed in the gun duel that follows. Like most scripts, however, this one had taken several drafts to get right—and because it had been written by a computer and not by a human, the network had decided to show a couple of the less successful versions as well.

The first of these had the robber, not the sheriff, winning the shoot-out—a plausible enough scenario in real life, if not in prime time. But in the second, TXO got caught in the same kind of endless loop that had incapacitated PANDORA. This time the robber's gun misfired and he fell into a loop spinning the chamber; the sheriff put his gun in the robber's holster and fell into a loop taking shots of whiskey. It ended like that, the robber endlessly spinning his gun chamber, the sheriff endlessly belting down shots of whiskey, like mindless robots caught in a reality-warp.

The reason loops like these occur is that loops are what most computer programs are made up of—not infinite loops, from which there's no escape, but more useful kinds of loops that keep the program pointed in the right direction. Computer programs usually consist of a series of instructions that have to be followed until some precondition is met. The computer follows these instructions in its very methodical, step-by-step fashion, and if the precondition isn't satisfied the first time around, the program keeps looping back again and again until it is. At that point the program either shuts itself off or enters another loop set up in the same fashion. There can be loops within loops, and loops within loops within loops.

PANDORA itself is nothing more than a long sequence of looped instructions. If any events occur, it's instructed to deal with them; if any goals pop up, it's instructed to plan for them; and if any plans are made, it's instructed to execute them. It keeps on doing this until all events have been processed, all goals planned for, and all plans executed. Then it stops—unless it slips into an infinite loop that prevents it from completing the series.

In this case, the unwelcome loop could be fixed by filling in the "effects" slot in the raincoat plan. Actually, however, it was a little more complicated than that. The effect of putting on a raincoat would be having a raincoat on, and then the demon RainCheck would have to be changed to tell PANDORA that it would get wet unless it had a raincoat on. That would be fine for raincoats, but what would happen when PANDORA was programmed to know about other ways of staying dry—umbrellas, for instance? Things could get complicated rather quickly, and Joe didn't want PANDORA to stay at the raincoat stage forever.

"My first goal is to get PANDORA to put on a raincoat," he explained. "After that, if it doesn't have a raincoat, I want it to think of going out and *buying* a raincoat—and then it has to realize that if it does that, it'll get wet. Hopefully it'll eventually get to the point where it decides to send the dog out, or else run. But to do that, it has to realize that getting wet is okay if you don't get *too* wet." He grinned. "Maybe it'll use the newspaper on the way back to cover its head."

To come up with solutions like these, PANDORA would need a far more sophisticated knowledge base than it had now. The problem was one of representation. How do you represent knowledge about raincoats and umbrellas and dogs and running in a way that all of it can be accessed when you wake up in the morning? At the moment, PANDORA's knowledge base consisted of nothing more than a few slot-fillers and some inference rules—that is, a few facts arranged fill-in-the-blanks-style and some rules that said, "If this, then that." But if it were to deal with raincoats and umbrellas, at the same time, it would need a much more efficient memory. How would you set up a memory? Joe wasn't sure. But he and Peter Norvig were working on the problem, and they thought it had something to do with frames.

On a Tuesday morning a couple of weeks after PANDORA's encounter with the raincoat, I walked into the AI office to find the whiteboard covered with messages about love.

These messages were not human-to-human; they were the rough draft of a detailed instruction set for Kim. Eventually this instruction set would form the basis of a frame-based memory system to be shared by the two sister programs, PAMELA and PANDORA—the story-understander and the problem-solver. Right now, however, there was nothing more than a diagram of a three-sentence love story involving two humans, John and Mary. "John loved Mary," the story read. "John asked Mary to marry him. Mary accepted."

On the right-hand side of the whiteboard, someone had drawn three large rectangles marked "Frames." One of these frames was labeled "Ask." The second was labeled "Planning." The third and largest was labeled "Love." Nested within the "Love" frame were three more frames: "Romantic Love," "Familial Love," and "Platonic Love." Nested inside the "Romantic Love" frame were three more: "Marriage," "Unrequited Love," and "Affair." The whole thing looked like this:

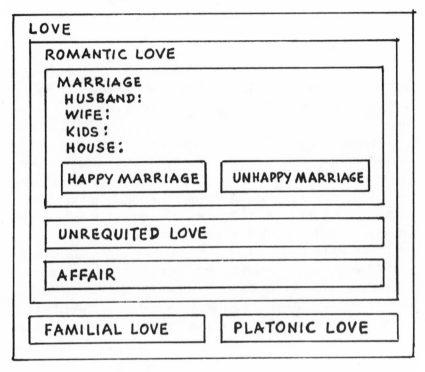

To the left of that were two lists. One list was marked "Assertions" and had items labeled a), b), c). The other was marked "Rules" and had items labeled 1), 2), 3), 4), 5), 6), 7). Above these lists was a diagram which looked like the directions to a Rube Goldberg construction:

"J loved M"
   triggers rule 1) which invokes frame LOVE
   this activates rules 4), 5) —
      4) invokes ROMANTIC LOVE which activates 6), 7)
      and asserts a), b) [perhaps a few more]

"J asked M to marry him"
  triggers 2) which invokes PLANNING
      3) which invokes ASK—more specific, so it wins
        which asserts c)
          which adds to 6), 7)
"M accepted"
  fulfills 6), eliminates 7)

In one corner of the whiteboard, Yigal's daughter had done a tiny stick-figure drawing of a little girl with a dog on a leash. This was a permanent fixture of the whiteboard. It didn't have anything to do with artificial intelligence.

"I'm trying to figure out the processes that are involved in doing understanding," Peter explained when I asked him about the rest of it. "One process that's involved is what I call 'frame invocation.'

"A frame is just an organized set of knowledge that you use to understand a specific situation. In Joe's problem, when you see it's raining out, then you want to bring in all this new knowledge. And one of the rules that you now worry about is 'If I go outside, then I'm going to get wet.' Before you knew it was raining, you never considered whether or not you would get wet.

"If you're just building a small program with a very small number of rules, then you could get away with having a program that checks every rule all the time. It's sunny out and you go outside, and it checks to see—is it raining? Will you get wet? And it would say no and it would continue on from there. The program would appear to work correctly because it didn't make any false assumptions, like the assumption that you were gonna get wet—but in fact it made a mistake just by even considering whether you would get wet when it's sunny.

"So you have to have a theory that will cut down on the number of things it will consider. That's one of the processes I'm working on—trying to figure out how to organize knowledge so that you'll get the knowledge you want when you need it, but you won't get too much of it when you don't need it."

So the idea was to build a mechanism that would invoke the right frames in the right order. The love story was a test. Their mechanism was supposed to work like this:

The first sentence—"John loves Mary"—triggers the rule that invokes the "Love" frame, and that in turn triggers two more rules that call up the subframes "Romantic Love" and "Familial Love." The "Romantic Love" subframe is invoked, triggering yet another pair of rules that call up the subframes "Marriage" and "Unrequited Love," and making the assertion that John has a high opinion of Mary and that he enjoys her company.

The second sentence—"John asked Mary to marry him"—triggers the rule that calls up the "Planning" frame and the rule that calls up the "Ask" frame. "Ask" is invoked, making the assertion that John has the goal of marrying Mary.

The final sentence—"Mary accepted"—fulfills the conditions for the "Marriage" frame and rules out the possibility that "Unrequited Love" will have to be invoked instead.

It wasn't the way love had ever been explained to me, but I wasn't a computer. And besides, Peter wasn't so much interested in explaining love as he was in figuring out how it gets understood —how the mind manipulates the symbols that are associated with love. "The specifics of what love is made up of—that's not really what's important," he said. "What's important is the way you do the processing. If you come up with a good model that does all the processing in the right way, then it would be fairly easy to display all the knowledge you need."

Peter and Joe had started working on this frame-based system a few weeks earlier. From their point of view, it was largely a design problem. The task was to design a working model of the human understanding process—a program that would take care of the automatic processing that comes between sensory input and the mental state we call "understanding." That meant constructing a model of the understanding process and then expressing that model as a series of algorithms, formal instructions so detailed as to enable a computer to reproduce this model precisely. The goal was to come up with a clean solution—an elegant piece of programming, something that could do the job with the least possible effort. They were mind engineers, using skills that most engineers never develop—programming skills, skills of introspection.

The introspective technique was something Wilensky had brought with him from Yale. How do you figure out how the mind works? You start with your own, and then you ask the people around you. Every year, Roger Schank gives a lecture in which the basic message is, "collect data." It isn't necessary to go about this as systematically as a psychologist or an anthropologist would, he says, but it is necessary to gather examples of the mind at work and to use them as the basis of your computer programs.

The practice of asking people to describe their own mental processes—an approach known as introspectionism—was used a century ago by the pioneers of psychology. By the Twenties, however, this technique had been found wanting. How valid were conjectures about your own subconscious? How could you examine your own mind? For the next forty years, psychological research was dominated by the behaviorist approach, which held that the workings of the mind could not be studied scientifically and probably weren't that important anyway. All that was necessary, the behaviorists maintained, was to study the input and the output—that is, conditioning and behavior. What went on inside could simply be ignored.

So powerful was the behaviorist mystique that for most of this century, few research psychologists even tried to figure out how the mind works. When they finally started it was in response to developments outside psychology—among them information theory, which held that a computer could process information in much the same way as the human mind. If the computer could be likened to the mind, some wondered, couldn't the mind be likened to a computer? And so arose the cognitive approach, which has lately replaced behaviorism as the fashion in academic psychology. If the behaviorists saw the human as an overgrown lab rat—as an animal to be conditioned at will—the cognitivists view the human as a fleshy computer—as a complex symbol-manipulating device to be examined and understood. The result is introspectionism with a high-technology twist, for what separates the cognitivists from their predecessors is computer technology. Cognitive researchers in AI and psychology seek to model the mind on a computer, and that demands a rigorous, step-by-step explanation of all its hidden workings. With the computer, vague theories and fuzzy-mindedness won't do. With the computer, precision prevails.

For Peter, the introspective technique was a novelty. Most of his skills were in programming and math. His father had been a mathematics professor, first at the University of Massachusetts, later at Wellesley. Peter had been a math major at Brown, where his father had done his graduate work. He liked math. He liked puzzles, and he liked the feeling you get from working on certain mathematical problems—the flash of insight, the fleeting yet powerful glimpse of the deep, underlying structure of mathematics. But he liked programming even better.

One reason he preferred programming was that he was better at it. Math was getting too hard too soon. Then he took an AI course and discovered MACSYMA, the MIT program that manipulates algebraic expressions. It was ridiculous. Here he was, slaving away on differential equations, and there was already a computer program that could do it faster. That was when he discovered you could make money writing other computer programs.

For Peter, the difference between mathematics and computer programming was the difference between a problem you could stare at for hours without result and a problem you could solve by trial and error. Programming was easy and fun. He'd taken his first computer course as a high-school student in the leafy Boston suburb of Newton—his father had moved to Wellesley by then—and even at that point he knew more than the teacher. By the time he was a senior at Brown, he was programming the computer for his roommate's dad's business. Then he graduated and got a job at a software firm in Cambridge, writing programs that automatically drew flow charts of other programs.

Peter spent two years in Cambridge. He was excited when he got there: It was a small company, informal, and they were paying him to do something he enjoyed. He was bored when he left. "I was dissatisfied with the working environment," he said. Part of it was the company he was working for—a military contractor whose ties to the Pentagon he found bothersome. And part of it was the nature of the work.

"The thing that's interesting about programming is getting a small problem and finding a solution to it—puzzles, Rubik's cube–type things. It's fine to do that, but then you get the feeling that that's all you're doing with your life, playing little games. That's what programming is like. How do you make that more interesting? Well, if you're building a program that has some meaning to society, or if you discover some theory that's useful to computer science, then that makes programming more interesting."

On his application to Berkeley, on the blank that asked for field of study, Peter wrote "AI." He wasn't sure it was what he wanted to do, but he did want to work with computers and he figured a year wouldn't hurt. He also figured that the school he'd really want to go to would be Stanford, because Stanford was the one with the big AI program and the famous people on the faculty. Then he met Wilensky.

This was in 1980, only two years after Wilensky had arrived from Yale. Stanford had two AI labs, both of them world-famous. One was headed by John McCarthy, one of the founding fathers of artificial intelligence; the other was headed by Edward Feigenbaum, the man who'd made it a commercial proposition. Between them, these two labs had perhaps a hundred researchers. There were carpets on the floors and candy machines that automatically billed your computer account. Berkeley had no carpets, no computerized candy-billing procedures, no big names—just Joe and Yigal and Wilensky and a couple of master's candidates. But Peter hadn't expected Wilensky to be so organized, so fast-talking, so aggressive.

"He tried to convince me that coming to Berkeley would actually be better for me than going to Stanford," Peter recalled, a trace of incredulity in his voice. "He was saying, 'Berkeley would be the best place in the world for you to go.' That wasn't what I'd expected to hear. But what he said was essentially correct, which was that if I wanted to work on natural language–type things, there's nobody at Stanford who's interested in doing it. They have a lot of money and facilities and a lot of people doing things that are called 'artificial intelligence,' but there's nobody doing the types of things that we're doing here."

The difference between Berkeley and Stanford is the difference between two visions of California: the utopian populist vision and the feudal agrarian vision—in its contemporary form, feudal corporate. Berkeley is a high-pressure vale of public scholarship on the edge of the Oakland ghetto. Stanford is an educational theme park, a vast technology ranch that sprawls alongside the perfectly manicured suburb of Palo Alto.

Cool and serene beneath the warm California sun, Stanford looks less like a college campus than like a philosopher's garden. A palm-lined boulevard runs arrow-straight through a wooded grove to the heart of it: a monastic cloister of Victorian stone buildings, tightly ordered, Romanesque in design, with a chapel in their center. A gentle mountain range rises in the background, and between the mountains and the chapel sits an enormous radio dish, its face turned heavenward to receive signals from alien civilizations. It is here, amid topiary and fountains, that some of America's most advanced computer research has been conducted.

Most of the AI work at Stanford has been in the fields of vision, robotics, and expert systems. During the Sixties, Feigenbaum pioneered expert systems with DENDRAL, the program that provides chemical analyses of organic compounds. Edward Shortliffe, a Stanford medical professor, employed the same principles to create MYCIN, the expert medical consultant. The essence of MYCIN—its logical-inference mechanism—was then extracted to form EMYCIN, a universal system that theoretically can be adapted to function in almost any expert domain.

Vision and robotics have been the main areas of exploration at SAIL, the lab John McCarthy set up with ARPA funding not long after he arrived in 1962. Researchers at the robotics lab have been working with Unimation, the leading American manufacturer of industrial robots, to develop a three-wheeled robot that can scoot about the factory, picking up widgets and feeding them to other machines. Another group has been working with the Veterans Administration on a personal-servant robot for the handicapped —a movable robot arm that can respond to voice commands to pick up a can of soda, say, or reach under a table for a pen that has rolled to the floor. The vision lab has produced a geometric modeling system that can pick out L-1011 jumbo jets in aerial photos of San Francisco Airport. Its goal is to produce a stereo vision system that can "see" in 3-D much like human eyes.

One of the few people thinking about common sense at Stanford is McCarthy himself. A striking-looking man, silver-haired and patriarchal with a wolfen beard, McCarthy has a face that suggests Charlton Heston's Moses in *The Ten Commandments*. He exhibits a startling and original intelligence, as well as a number of disconcerting social habits—a tendency to walk away from conversations in midsentence, for example. These are generally accepted as the prerogatives of a great thinker.

In the very early days of AI, when his contemporaries were claiming great success with theorem-proving programs and chess-playing programs, it was McCarthy who suggested that the true secrets of intelligence might be more elusive. In 1958 he predicted that common sense would be the stumbling block, and ever since then he's been working to remove it. But the method he's taken is radically different from the Schankian approach, for he views common sense as something that happens according to the rigid precepts of mathematical logic—as theorem-proving, essentially. Success has so far eluded him, but he remains hopeful. "As far as I'm concerned," he told Pamela McCorduck in *Machines Who Think*, her history of the field, "this is *the* key unsolved problem in AI."

But at Stanford, the real thrust was elsewhere. AI at Stanford was practical and real—and somewhat modest in its expectations. AI at Berkeley was bold and audacious. Stanford was offering useful tools. Berkeley was holding out the dream of the intelligent machine.

In the end, the question of Berkeley or Stanford became a moot point for Peter. Along with 75 percent of Stanford's graduate-level engineering applicants, he was turned down. It didn't matter; at that point, he didn't know enough to choose between them anyway.

During Peter's second quarter at Berkeley, Wilensky gave him PAM to look at. PAM's reputation as a story-understander was based on its knowledge of goals and the way goals interact. Given a story, it could examine the characters' actions and figure out why they did what they did. This is one component of understanding. Peter decided to try some others.

At that point, Joe's friend Mike Deering had already rigged up a couple of extensions to PAM. One of them took care of "story points"—the idea that there are important points to any story, and that to summarize the story you need to pick them out. The other implemented the meta-planning theory Wilensky described in his *Cognitive Science* paper. Meta-planning enabled PAM to deal with really complicated goal interactions—not just multiple goals, but multiple goal conflicts. Using it, PAM could not only figure out a character's goals, it could figure out how that character might change his behavior as new goals stacked up. If it heard that a man wanted to go out with his secretary but didn't want his wife to know—to pick an example from the paper—it would be able to understand why he might call his wife to say he'd be working late in the office.

Peter looked at all this and started to streamline it a bit. Then he decided that instead of modifying someone else's program, he'd do better to start from scratch. He decided to try to build a more general understanding system. To do that, he realized, he'd have to give it knowledge about more than just goals. One thing he'd have to give it was the capacity to be reminded of things. Why do we associate some things with other things—bees with flowers, sofas with chairs, love with marriage? How does that mechanism work in humans? How should it work in a computer program? That's what Peter wanted to know.

PAM didn't have this ability to make associations. If you asked PAM why John had asked Mary to marry him, it would say it was because he was in love with her. It wouldn't say anything else because it wouldn't really know what love means. It would not have what Peter called "a large number of assertions about what it means to love." PAMELA would, if Joe and Peter could get their frame-based memory system to work. PAMELA would hear about marriage and think of wedding rings and rice and white lace and honeymoons and baby carriages, just as a human would. PAMELA would make what Joe called the "unconscious connections."

"The things that PAM would do were more the conscious types of things," Peter said. "If you asked it, 'What did you understand about this story?' it would be able to list out exactly what the story was about. But when you hear a story, you're put into a certain frame of mind where a whole lot of background knowledge has been brought in. If you were told to repeat what's in the story, you might not mention that. Why wouldn't you mention it? Well, one reason is because you might assume the other person would be in the same frame of mind and you don't have to."

The mechanism Peter and Joe had been testing on the "John loves Mary" story would give PAMELA and PANDORA, for the first time, a fully realized, frame-based memory. Just as it would enable PANDORA to think of raincoats and unbrellas simultaneously, so it would enable PAMELA to respond to the word "marriage" with a whole flood of associations. As soon as they could get this mechanism working, they were planning to incorporate it into their programs. "We've been conceptualizing for a month or so," Peter said. "I think we'll be ready to write code in a week."

It was early in the afternoon, and various members of the AI team were scurrying in and out—dropping in between classes, heading off for seminars, coming in to work on their programs. Marc was at one of the terminals, working on a programming assignment for CS 284, Wilensky's graduate-level course in AI programming techniques. He raised his head and gave Peter a quizzical look. "You said that six months ago," he said. Peter looked sheepish and grinned.

A week later, at 2:30 on a Friday afternoon, Joe was parked at a terminal, writing code. He and Peter had been up until 3:30 that morning setting up frames for the "John loves Mary" story. They'd gotten part of it to work: Now when you typed in "John loves Mary," it automatically invoked the Romantic Love frame. This happens unconsciously in humans. Now it was happening in their understanding mechanism as well.

Only Joe and Yigal were at the office this afternoon. Yigal was working at the other terminal. The blinds on the window were raised. Outside, a couple of undergraduates were strolling across the park on the roof of the Bechtel Engineering Center, a plush new lounge-and-library building put up for engineering students by the Bechtel Corporation, the giant San Francisco–based engineering firm. Beyond Bechtel—a ground-hugging structure, environmentally sensitive, low-profile—rose the blank concrete facade of Davis Hall, topped incongruously by a Spanish-style red tile roof. Beyond Davis rose the Berkeley Hills, deep green at this time of year, studded with houses. Low clouds hung behind the hills, with a clear blue sky above.

The only thing the understanding mechanism knew about love

was that it was something called an "attitude." An attitude was something called a "mental object." These and other facts had been stored in its knowledge base in a precise and orderly fashion:

```
;  Concepts are questions, states, objects,
;    events or general knowledge
(create base Concept)
(create expanded Concept Object)
;  Objects are physical or mental.
;    Physical objects are books, places, etc.
(create expanded Object PhysicalObject)
(create expanded PhysicalObject AnimateObject)
(create expanded AnimateObject Person)
(create expanded Person Man)
(create expanded Person Woman)
;  Mental objects are goals, attitudes,
     beliefs, etc.
(create expanded object MentalObject
  (Planner Person))
(create expanded MentalObject Attitude
  (Towards Concept))
(create expanded Attitude Love)
```

So this is what it's like to educate a computer, I thought—as if you could just open up a person's head and pour knowledge inside in the form of declarative statements, and then get it all to work by simply uttering commands.

"Educate a computer? That's what we're trying to do," Joe said. "But it's harder than that, because when you educate a human, you don't have to figure out what they're doing inside their head. You just have to tell them things, and somehow they do all the remembering automatically. But here we have to figure out how things should be stored and how connections get made. And we're trying to build a system that's already learned these things as opposed to doing the teaching ourselves, because having these structures built automatically is just too much to ask for."

The story Joe and Peter were working on was expressed in the same terms as the facts in the knowledge base. "John loves Mary" was represented as John has the attitude of love toward Mary. "John proposed to Mary" became John MTransed to Mary the question, Does she want to be in the state of being married to him? "Mary accepted" was Mary MTransed to John something positive. Exactly what was not spelled out.

In setting up their frames—what the memory system knows as FrameKnowledge—Joe and Peter had made a distinction between characteristics and defining features. A characteristic is something you might expect to find in a given frame; a defining feature is something that has to be there. A defining feature of the ManLovesWoman frame (as the Romantic Love frame was described in code) is that a man loves a woman. A characteristic of the ManLoves Woman frame is that both the man and the woman are adults. Anytime the system hears about love, it checks to see if it's love between a man and a woman. If it is, the ManLovesWoman frame is automatically invoked.

Now that they'd gotten the ManLovesWoman frame invoked, Joe was working on the Ask frame. The Ask frame would be full of knowledge about asking questions and getting answers. Joe was setting it up so that whenever it got invoked, it would automatically start looking for an answer. That meant looking for an MTrans, and as soon as it found one it would grab it to fill the empty slot.

"Eventually," Joe said, "we need to include the Proposal frame, too—the idea of proposing to someone—but we haven't thought that far ahead." He leaned back in his chair and clasped his hands behind his head. "That's actually going to be something for Peter to worry about. I'll have to worry about it, too, in the sense that if I wanted PANDORA to respond in the right way to a proposal of marriage, she would need to have the same knowledge—but that's too tough a question now for PANDORA. Nice practical things like putting her raincoat on are about all she can do."

Joe went to work at the terminal. Yigal wandered out. After an hour of typing, Joe sat up in his chair, smiled at the screen, and punched a couple of buttons to run the "John loves Mary" story again. The program flashed before him in green phosphorescent letters as it worked its way through the story. He sat at attention, eyes locked on the screen, muttering under his breath. Suddenly he crumpled and buried his face in his hands. *"Oh, no, no!"* he cried. "It thinks the question was the answer!"

It thinks the question was the answer?

"It couldn't tell the difference between the two MTranses—the question and the answer." Joe sat up and tried to pull himself together.

"I said the answer can be any old MTrans, and that's why it does it. I've got to figure out some way to say it can't be the question, it's got to be something that really would be the answer. Essentially I'm back to a representation problem. The thing is, how do I say that this has to be the answer to the question and not just any old MTrans?"

He slumped down in his chair, legs stretched out under the desk, hands folded under his chin, staring disconsolately at the screen. "Oh, gee," he said, "I don't even know where to start."

6

What Computers
Can't Do

Some twenty years before, Hubert Dreyfus had more or less predicted this remark. More precisely, he had predicted an infinite number of such remarks. Then a junior philosophy instructor at MIT, he was working on a paper for the Rand Corporation, a paper called "Alchemy and Artificial Intelligence." As the title implied, Dreyfus thought AI was a waste of time, a blind alley of science.

In 1972, after he'd moved to Berkeley, Dreyfus came out with his book, *What Computers Can't Do: The Limits of Artificial Intelligence*. What computers can't do, he argued, is think like people. They can't think like people because there's no way to represent all the background knowledge of ordinary human life —the stuff we associate with common sense—in some form a computer can understand. This background knowledge is something every human shares, and yet it cannot be formalized—that is, described so precisely and explicitly that it could serve as a set of instructions in a computer program. People who try, Dreyfus concluded, might as well be trying to turn lead into gold.

Dreyfus's attack on AI was radical and across-the-board. He ridiculed the early cognitive-simulation efforts at Carnegie Tech and MIT—the automatic theorem provers, the automatic chess players, the would-be automatic translators. He attacked the ad-hoc "semantic information-processing" approach that Marvin

Minsky pioneered in the Sixties. In a revised edition that appeared in 1979, he jeered at the artificially limited "microworlds" approach of the early Seventies, which assumed that if you could get a program to function in some finite environment, you could extend it to deal with the real world. Nor did he see success in the cards for the Schankian efforts at knowledge representation that had become prominent by the end of the decade.

Dreyfus was particularly scathing about some of the claims AI researchers have made—claims that do look extravagant in hindsight. In 1957, for example, Herbert Simon of Carnegie Tech predicted that in ten years a computer would be the world chess champion. A quarter century later it still hadn't happened—although Richard Greenblatt, a legendary hacker at MIT, did succeed in building a chess-playing program called MacHack that beat Dreyfus in 1964 and that went on to become an honorary member of the U.S. Chess Federation. Simon also predicted that in the not-too-distant future, computers would be able to handle any problem a human could deal with. This hadn't happened either, and Dreyfus did not fail to point it out.

But Dreyfus was attacking more than just AI; he was attacking a philosophical tradition that goes back to Plato. "According to Plato," he wrote, "all knowledge must be stateable in explicit definitions which anyone could apply." For this to be accomplished, any appeal to judgment and intuition would have to be eliminated. Just as Galileo succeeded in finding a pure formalism to describe physical motion, a "Galileo of human behavior" might reduce the whole of human knowledge to a single formal system. Leibniz, Dreyfus suggested, saw himself as just such a person:

> Leibniz thought he had found a universal and exact system of notation, an algebra . . . by means of which "we can assign to every object its determined characteristic number." In this way . . . all knowledge could be expressed and brought together in one deductive system. On the basis of these numbers and the rules for their combination all problems could be solved and all controversies ended: "if someone should doubt my results," Leibniz said, "I would say to him: 'Let us calculate, Sir,'

and thus by taking pen and ink, we should settle the question."*

Three hundred years later, however, the answer to this particular question—can human experience be formalized?—remains uncalculated. As a phenomenologist—a partisan of the twentieth-century Continental school of philosophy that culminated in the existentialism of Jean-Paul Sartre—Dreyfus holds that it never will be.

Phenomenology, as developed around the turn of the century by the German Edmund Husserl, is the study of pure phenomena —mental acts, which according to Husserl are all that give meaning to the world. It is an inquiry into the essence of things, an essence that Husserl felt can be understood only through the rigorous application of intuition. In Husserl's phrase, it is "an intuition of essences."

Even for philosophy, this was an abstract notion. But it was as nothing next to the writings of Husserl's pupil, Martin Heidegger, who supplanted him at the University of Freiburg under the Nazis. Heidegger, who's regarded even by his fellows as almost totally inscrutable, proclaimed an existential phenomenology— an inquiry into "the essence of being." Like Husserl, he sought to examine mental phenomena without any preconceptions. But he felt Husserl had made two key mistakes. First, Husserl had failed to rid himself of one fundamental preconception—the notion that the mind operates according to internal representations. Second, he'd failed to consider the fact of "being in the world"—a phrase Dreyfus takes to refer to the background of human existence. This background, this core of unspoken assumptions about what it means to be a human on Earth, is what Dreyfus is saying will forever resist formalization.

Heidegger saw his work as a radical departure from the philosophical tradition that stretched unbroken from Plato to Leibniz to Husserl. "Philosophy is ending in the present age," he wrote in "The End of Philosophy and the Task of Thinking." "It has found its place in the scientific attitude." Dreyfus agrees. As a

*Hubert L. Dreyfus, *What Computers Can't Do: The Limits of Artificial Intelligence* (Revised Edition), New York: Harper & Row, 1979, p. 69.

follower of Heidegger and of Maurice Merleau-Ponty, a French phenomenologist who likewise rebelled against Husserl, he believes that Husserl unwittingly revealed the problem with seeking any rigorous explanation for the mind—the impossibility of ever devising a formal representation for the totality of human experience. Since the notion of formal representation is at the core of artificial intelligence and cognitive science alike, Dreyfus believes that both are doomed to failure.

It was with some interest, then, that the scholars at Berkeley gathered that spring for the cognitive-science colloquium at which Dreyfus would give his talk on formalism.

The IHL Library was considerably less grand than the question that was being considered in it. Its flimsy walls offered faint support for a blackboard white with chalk dust. A couple of plywood tables had been pushed together in front of the blackboard, and about twenty-five student desks were scattered in a jumble in front of them. The door opened out onto a rickety stairway leading half a flight down to the ground—a stairway that might once have been painted gray, but now was peeling and splintered.

Shortly after two on a Tuesday afternoon, Dreyfus took his seat behind the table. A small, wiry man, he was wearing dark brown corduroy pants and a western-style plaid shirt. A brilliant shock of carrot-colored hair flourished about his head, and a pair of large, square, tortoiseshell glasses sat perched on his nose. He had the air of a passionate man.

Wilensky was out of town, but Joe, Yigal, Marc, and Peter were sitting side by side at the student desks. Other members of the AI group were scattered around nearby, interspersed with their counterparts from other fields—grad students in psychology, philosophy, linguistics. The seats at the table were taken up by senior faculty members. Almost everyone was wearing scruffy pants. No one was wearing a tie. There were a lot of beards, and not many women.

Dreyfus prefaced his remarks by modestly noting that he didn't claim to have the final word on formalism. "But as far as I can see," he declared, "to formalize is to isolate some sort of context-free elements. That's all there is to it." He shrugged and offered a smile.

"These elements come with lots of different names," he continued, "but whatever they are, they always turn out to be something that you can pick out without any reference to judgment, intuition, interpretation, or context. You can just *pick it out*—and a good test would be whether you can get a computer to just *pick it out*—and then you put these elements together in complex concatenations, and with this you try to capture the structure of whatever it is you're trying to study."

Dreyfus's voice was nasal and high-pitched, but with a resonance that left no doubt about his assertiveness. He had good timing as well. He sounded a bit like Jack Benny, although without Jack Benny's subject matter.

"Now, I don't think that's very illuminating, but you can see more what formalizing comes to if you ask yourself what formal*ism* is, and what is sacrificed to formalism. I think formalism is the claim that we can and must formalize whatever it is we're trying to understand, even what on the face of it is not amenable to formalizing. I mean, formalism is sort of fanatical formalizing, like cognitivism is fanatical cognitive science and communism is—et cetera. I mean, formalism is just pushing this idea of formalizing to the limit."

A rumble arose from the room. Even at Berkeley, it wasn't every day you heard formalism and communism discussed in the same breath. Dreyfus took no notice.

"Now you can begin to see what is sacrificed and what is gained. First, since it's my *favorite* subject, I'll talk about what's sacrificed." He rubbed his hands and gave a Jack Benny smile. "What's sacrificed is at least a lot of *prima facie* phenomena."

This set off an audible groan.

"Well, of course they're going to have to be saved somehow," Dreyfus responded, "but to begin with, what's left out are moods, feelings, et cetera, which don't even seem to be amenable to this sort of analysis. Also, images, similarity, prototypicality, and meaning—whatever that is. Now of course you *can't* leave all these out—they make up too much of the phenomena we want to study. So formalism is obviously the thesis that these can be *reduced* to concatenations of these context-free features."

In the hour that followed, Dreyfus went through the list of phenomena being studied. Vision—can images be viewed as logical concatenations of features? Skills—can they be formalized as a set of rules or instructions? Moods and feelings—they resist the formal treatment, so they just get tossed out as irrelevant. And what about similarity, the ability to recognize patterns? Dreyfus mentioned a gestalt psychologist who claims to have shown that people see certain patterns as similar even though they don't contain identical features—a result that would show the formalist view to be wrong.

"Now the logic of this whole thing," he continued, "is that there are a whole lot of *prima facie* phenomena in our experience—skills, moods, images, similarity, meaning—that don't look like they're amenable to this kind of formal analysis. And then there's a lot of *heavy going* trying to show that they can be so analyzed anyway. And then a lot of research and a lot of counterexamples, and more research and more counterexamples, and so the question arises, Why are people so busy *trying?* Why is formalism such an attractive option?

"I think that's *really* a fascinating question. I think you've got to go back to the whole philosophical tradition to get any kind of answer to that. And as far as I can see, what would be gained if we could pull off the formalist reduction would be that we would be able to have a *theory* and we would be able to have an *explanation.* In a way, that's what we're committed to. Nobody will be happy unless they have a theory and an explanation."

Dreyfus gave a thoroughly exasperated look. After all, it wasn't just any theory they wanted; it was a formal theory. "A *formal* theory is a theory that you could put on a computer because it would be completely explicit. A computer doesn't share our interpretations, our feelings, our background practices, our sense of when everything else is equal and when it isn't. But the attraction of having *nothing hidden,* of making *no appeal* even to our humanity, of having *everything explicit,* goes clear back to Plato! Plato already saw the intellectual beauty of it; then, in 1600, Galileo showed the incredible power of it; and now, naturally, everybody would like to have a completely explicit, formalizable theory."

During the question-and-answer exchange that followed, one student—an unabashed formalist—tried to compare Dreyfus to the cardinals of the Inquisition, those enemies of science who argued that the earth couldn't move around the sun because that contradicted the Scriptures. People began to titter, but Dreyfus was not even momentarily taken aback. "No, no!" he cried. "I'm arguing much more like the cardinals than that! The cardinals were very smart, but that wasn't a very smart argument.

"The cardinals were also saying to Galileo, 'Look, *prima facie*, things aren't like that. We can see the sun moving around the earth. You are flying in the face of the phenomena.' And Galileo was saying, 'So much the worse for the phenomena.' And that *worked* in science, and it's certainly the goal of cognitivism that we can do the same thing. But what I'm saying like the cardinals is that it's not obvious that the context is just a bunch of features that we have not yet recognized, that similarity is—"

"But what do you mean by 'context' if you don't mean extra features?"

"Well, how about asking me the other? What do I mean by 'similarity' if I don't mean extra—"

"No! Answer the question! What do you mean by 'context' if you don't mean extra features?"

"Okay. What I mean by 'context' is what you appeal to when you say, 'Everything else being equal.' And not only does it not seem *obvious* to me that the context is all made up out of facts and features, it seems *unintelligible* to me that the context is all made up out of facts and features—because you couldn't even pick out a fact or a feature except in terms of this background of everything else being equal. That's how it looks to me."

The comparison of the cognitive scientists with Galileo and of Dreyfus with the cardinals in Rome was not as fanciful as it might sound. It was Galileo—astronomer, physicist, mathematician—who laid the foundations for the scientific investigation of the physical world. He did this by combining experimentation with mathematical formalism. "The Book of Nature," he wrote in 1623, "is written in mathematical characters." It was a radical notion for his time.

Mathematics provided a seductive tool, a language powerful enough to describe with precision what the experiments suggested. In order to use this tool, however, certain sacrifices had to be made. Subjective properties were not amenable to mathematical description. Subjective properties were deemed to have little usefulness in describing the physical world.

The power of mathematics was sufficient to enable Newton to solve the mysteries of celestial motion and thus come up with a model of the universe. With his fundamental laws of mechanics, Newton provided the first systematic explanation of a world that had always seemed mystical and veiled. He explained the unexplained. He did it in a way that was rational and reassuring. He created a vision of a world existing in absolute space and absolute time, operating as a clocklike mechanism according to natural and immutable laws. God had set it all in motion, and now it was operating according to His plan.

This is not, we know now, the world we live in. But it resembles the real world closely enough to have changed civilization altogether. It gave us the Enlightenment and the Industrial Revolution. It gave us the ideas the United States was founded on—the political philosophy of John Locke, the economic philosophy of Adam Smith. But most important, it gave Western humanity a sense, for more than two centuries at least, that reality was predictable and comprehensible.

This is what formal theory does: It postulates order in a seemingly random universe; it gives structure to our experience; it reassures us that our world is understandable and hence, in some deep sense, okay. In attacking formal theories of the mind, Dreyfus is saying that there are things about the mind which we will never understand. This is a position some people find deeply upsetting.

There was one way the comparison of Dreyfus with the cardinals didn't hold up. In Rome, Galileo had been alone against a multitude of cardinals. At Berkeley, it was Dreyfus who was alone, facing a roomful of cognitive scientists. Times had changed.

In the three and a half centuries since Galileo's trial, science had explored and explained almost every aspect of the physical world, from the infinitely large to the infinitesimally small. Applied to the structure of the atom, the formal, reductionist view had proven explosive, apocalyptic. Now science was proposing to apply this same tool to the mind—to reduce mental phenomena to their essential features, just as physical phenomena have been reduced to waves of dancing particles. But this was a different

91

proposition, for the mind is not part of the physical world. The mind exists beyond the physical. It's not just the neurons, it's what the neurons do. It's invisible, intangible, unknown—and perhaps, as Dreyfus would say, unknowable.

"Let's say you take a look at mind," said Wilensky, leaning forward over his desk. We were discussing the virtues of science. "Now, what's happened as you go back over history is that as things in philosophy got better, they stopped being philosophy. If you're interested in the physical world, you don't go to a philosopher anymore. The same is true for questions about life—you go to a biologist for that. So what's left in philosophy? Well, a few things—things like ethics and the mind."

It was late in the afternoon, not long after Dreyfus's talk. Wilensky was in his office, logged into Kim, writing his book. Out the window behind him, the Berkeley Hills rose in a solid green wall. Barely visible between the trees was Cyclotron Road, a twisting trail that leads to the Lawrence Berkeley Lab—the sprawling hilltop complex that serves as a living memorial to Ernest O. Lawrence, Nobel laureate, atom splitter, father of "big science."

"I've always kind of believed there was something better about science than about other things," Wilensky continued. "I really am a scientific chauvinist in this respect. I'm not sure that philosophy, as it exists distinct from science, has made continuous contributions to our understanding of the world, or that history has improved and we now understand history in some way that we didn't ten years ago. But I think in science that we do understand the physical world, for example, better than we did a hundred years ago. And one of the reasons I always thought there was tension between philosophers and AI people is that you could claim that some of AI is doing to the study of the mind what physics and chemistry have done to the study of the physical world. What if it's possible to apply the same sort of rigor to describing how the mind works as it is to describing how the physical world works?"

I remarked that Dreyfus seems to be suggesting that this time science has met its match. Wilensky grinned and started fiddling with a pencil.

"One of the best things to have is people who disagree with

you," he said. "I get along with Bert just fine. I find him to be wrong about a lot of things, but I find him to be not that unreasonable. Actually, it's gotten to the point now where in many ways my position and his aren't all that different."

I must have looked surprised.

"Years ago, well before I ever got into this game, there was a tendency to think in terms of a few general principles that would give rise to a wondrous, intelligent being. The subsequent finding, if you will, was that it ain't like that at all. Most people are a lot less optimistic that AI is right around the corner. There's a lot of hard work ahead of us. So in a sense, Dreyfus's position today is a whole lot closer to the current mainstream AI position.

"If you set me down in a room with Bert, we'll have the following conversation. He'll say, 'If you want AI to work, you're gonna have to take all this knowledge and formalize it.' And I'll go, 'That's right.' And he'll say, 'And you'll have to shove it inside the machine.' And I'll go, 'That's right.' And he'll say, 'And you're gonna have to organize it, and you're gonna have to figure out what's appropriate for what situation, and there's a whole huge amount of it!' And I'll go, 'That's right!' And he'll say, 'And you can't do it!' And I'll go, 'Well, maybe you can.'" There was a sly drawl in his voice.

"The difference is whether or not you think it's going to be very, very hard to do all this, or whether you think it's going to be so hard that it's impossible. Certainly there are some things that are formalizable and some things that resist it more and more. But where do you draw the line? And can you continue pushing the line further and further? And if you can't, why not? Those are the interesting questions, and my real objection to Dreyfus is, why say at this stage that it's gonna fail?

"It's like saying, 'Well, you just can't talk about human life in terms of chemistry, and any attempts to *reduce* human life to chemistry will fail.' There's a sense in which that's right—humans are probably too complicated to give a good accounting of them in terms of biochemistry. It doesn't mean it's in principle wrong to try. It doesn't say, 'Look, you shouldn't do biochemistry because in principle it's going to leave out what we know about human beings in some mystical way.'

"An analogous question would be, Can you build a person? And the answer is, *'Oy!'* I mean, you can't even build an amoeba because it's so complicated. But that's not because you can't do it in principle. And maybe what we'll have will be the analogous kind of thing—that we can tamper with this and build things based on the principles we discover about how it all works, and they won't look exactly like humans and they won't be quite as complicated, but they will have some of the interesting properties humans have.

"But personally and all that, I get along with Dreyfus very well." Wilensky paused for a moment and chuckled. "You know, one of the people here got very much caught up in all this Buddhist stuff a while back—Naropa, Tibetan Buddhism, all that. It's not my cup of tea, but I didn't know that then. They had a meeting during the summer at Naropa, which is in Boulder, on 'Contrasting Perspectives in Cognitive Science,' and they invited five of us to come up there. And their view was so far removed from reality from my point of view that Bert and I ended up agreeing on *everything,* and they ended up identifying him as a *Western scientist.*

"There was one point at which they were talking about how science people have aggressive tendencies and this causes them to distort—or whatever it is they were saying, and Bert made some comment and they objected to him in a way that made it clear that they were classifying him as being one of these Western scientists who believe that there is objectivity and you have to have emotional detachment from your work. And he jumped up and he said, *'No!* I am *not* a *scientist!* I am an *existential philosopher!* I put my ego into everything I do and I *like aggression!'* And they had no idea how to react to that at all. So I just loved him for it."

Wilensky grinned and leaned back in his chair. "No, I get quite a charge out of Bert. He's such an authentic human being. I just wish he'd leave us alone already!"

Hubert Dreyfus was sitting behind his desk in his office in Moses Hall, a citadel of philosophy on the other side of the Campanile from Evans. Moses is a castlelike little structure that bristles with battlements but is nonetheless overshadowed by the new tabernacle of computation and mathematics. Dreyfus's office, which is beige with pink woodwork, looks directly over at it. He had his feet tucked inside one of the desk drawers. I asked him what had motivated him to take on AI in the first place, back in the early Sixties.

"I was teaching at MIT," he said, "and I was being told by Minsky's students that we philosophers were out-of-date—that these problems of what understanding is and what perception is had been solved or were about to be solved by the people in the AI lab. The philosophers I was teaching at that time—Merleau-Ponty and Heidegger—are still my main philosophers, and if you understood the implications of their work, it followed that a formal model of these processes shouldn't be possible. So it was kind of a challenge to me. If the AI people were right, then my favorite philosophers were wrong; and if my favorite philosophers were right, then the AI people were heading up a blind alley. But there was nothing I could do about it except for luck." He grinned with the recollection and dug his feet deeper into the drawer.

The luck came in the form of Dreyfus's brother, Stuart, who was then a mathematician at the Rand Corporation, the onetime air-force think tank in Santa Monica. Stuart Dreyfus was then a proponent of formal modeling. Now an operations-research specialist at Berkeley (operations research is a branch of engineering that deals with man-machine systems), he has become, in his brother's words, "a better phenomenologist than I am."

"Rand is where the big, important AI work was being done," Dreyfus continued. "Newell and Simon were at Rand writing papers like mad on understanding and intuition and problem-solving and chess-playing, and my brother was already very suspicious. He had no presuppositions—in fact, as a formal mathematician, he thought in general like they did. He just thought they were doing shoddy science.

"But then came this bit of luck. I wrote to him and I said, 'Look, Merleau-Ponty and the people I teach say that the stuff that's being done at Rand is wrongheaded.' He showed this letter to a guy at Rand, who said, 'What a strange thing! My brother just wrote me from Israel saying he's reading Merleau-Ponty, and Merleau-Ponty would be critical of this kind of stuff.' Just an incredible coincidence.

"So the two of them got Rand to hire me as a consultant to come and read Merleau-Ponty and Newell and Simon. I spent a summer at Rand and I read all the stuff they had and I wrote my paper. Then Papert [Seymour Papert, an associate of Minsky's at MIT, the man who invented the children's computer language LOGO] wrote his answer, called 'The Artificial Intelligence of Hubert L. Dreyfus,' and Rand held a meeting and discussed it, and the Russians held a meeting in Novosibirsk and discussed it, and I got all this funny feedback.

"But I was hooked on it from the first week at Rand, when I read Newell and Simon. On the one hand, I was angry about it because I thought it was shoddy and pretentious; and on the other hand, I was fascinated because it was the culmination of philosophy. Philosophy really has reached its culmination in artificial intelligence. They've inherited it."

I had to admit confusion. Was philosophy really over? And if so, what were we doing here?

Dreyfus tried to explain. "What happens is that Plato invents the idea of theory, and philosophy also starts with Plato, so philosophy is all tied up with the power of theory. Philosophy was set up so that it's quite natural all the sciences would branch off from it. And now there's this last question, What is the mind? It's finally going over into science, and that's cognitive science.

"But people like Heidegger say that philosophers from Plato on have neglected something else that is more fundamental than theory, which is a certain taken-for-granted background of shared practices and meanings that set up the possibility of any kind of science. Wittgenstein and Heidegger share the view that philosophy is over, because philosophy is practically defined by the forgetting of this background.

"So if you define philosophy as the forgetting of this background, then you've got to say that philosophy is now finished. And with this new thing that Heidegger calls 'thinking,' we're going to study what this background is, how it works, what meaning is, and how meaning is in the background. That's what I'm doing, you see. It just happens to be in the philosophy department.

"As Heidegger puts it, philosophy is finished because it's reached its culmination in technology. Now it's the job of the technologists, and there's nothing more for philosophers to do.

They have gradually turned the whole world into a possible object for theory. Of course, you could still go on debaung issues like causality, but they seem arcane and irrelevant to most people, I'm afraid, including me. So I'm saying that philosophy is over, and that these people have inherited a lemon."

$$7$$

PHRAN and PHRED

Within a few days, Joe and Peter had found a solution to the question-and-answer problem they'd encountered in the John-loves-Mary story. It was just a quick-and-dirty fix, but it would work until they could come up with something better. If the system couldn't tell the difference between John's proposal and Mary's answer because all it knew to look for was an MTrans, they could kludge it so the question wasn't there when the program went looking for the answer. It still wouldn't be able to tell a question from an answer, but this time it wouldn't need to.

The real solution, of course, would have to be a lot more sophisticated than that. The real solution would have to involve a precise explanation of what a question is, what an answer is, and how to tell a bad answer from a good answer for any particular question. But that would have to wait, because first Joe and Peter wanted to figure out how to invoke the Marriage frame and the Proposal frame.

In order for a frame to be invoked, something had to trigger it. Their system was set up so that if it heard about somebody getting married, that automatically triggered the Marriage frame. If it heard about somebody proposing, that automatically triggered the Proposal frame. It ought to trigger the Marriage frame as well, since a proposal is a step in the plan for getting married, and hearing about a proposal is likely to bring to mind the knowledge you have about marriage. But how, exactly, do you draw the connection between proposal and marriage? It certainly seems automatic in people. And yet when Joe and Peter tried to model it in their frame-based memory system, they ran into trouble.

They spent all one morning drawing diagrams on the whiteboard, trying to figure it out. The problem was that at this point there was only one way their system could invoke a frame—by stumbling across it directly. If you said "marry," it would invoke the Marriage frame. If you said "propose," it would invoke the Proposal frame. But if you said "propose"—as in "John proposed to Mary"—there was no way it would invoke the Marriage frame. It was too complicated. They didn't know how to do it.

Then they decided it wasn't the proposal itself that invoked the Marriage frame, it was the content of the proposal—the question "Will you marry me?" The word *marry* invoked the Marriage frame and all the right connections were made. Then they decided to represent the Proposal frame as a "precisification"—one of Peter's favorite words—of the Ask frame, rather than as a frame of its own. But then they ran into another problem, because when they set up the Ask frame and the Proposal frame, they made the mistake of having them point to each other. Propose was a precisification of Ask, and Ask was a generalization of Propose, and that caused the whole system to tumble into a loop. At that point they decided that they were tired and that maybe they should just quit for the afternoon.

It was not a pretty day. Unseasonable rains had battered the Bay Area all week. Shoes were soggy, spirits drenched. Dark gray clouds hungs low over the hills. Peter headed out the office door. Joe remained, logged in on Kim. Margaret walked in and announced that she'd just been talking to a grad student in the terminal room when a professor walked in and started talking about how all undergraduates are stupid—as if she weren't even there.

Yigal was reading his electronic mail on the ARPAnet, the high-speed computer communications network set up by the Pentagon to link its military bases with corporate and academic research centers. Messages on the ARPAnet could be flashed around the world instantaneously—and not just messages but complex diagrams as well, for the ARPAnet had been set up to facilitate development of the VHSIC chip, the very high-speed integrated circuit that's expected to be a key element in the electronic warfare of the future. Unfortunately, security on the ARPAnet was so lax that the system was quite regularly penetrated by high-school students logging in on their home computers.* A fundamentalist chain letter had made the rounds a couple of months earlier: Acknowledge God and He will light your way, ignore this message and you will die. This brought a stern warning from a major in the Pentagon—but nobody could be sure it really *was* from a major in the Pentagon, because anybody could have sent the message. Still, as Yigal pointed out, "It's a lot faster than the U.S. mail—or as someone called it on this thing once, 'Snail Mail.' "

Joe was stretched out in his old oak office chair, elbows on the chair arms, back to the window. A terminal was perched on the tiny desk beside him. He was wearing navy-and-white checked pants and a navy-and-white sweater with a dramatic V pattern down the front of it. The effect was startling—busy, yet precise.

This weekend he was planning to drive up to Lake Tahoe with his parents and his aunt and uncle. They were going to see the Captain and Tennille in concert, and Joe was going to watch his dad win money in the casinos. When he came back, he and Peter would have to settle this question of frame invocation.

"The other problem we've been putting off," he said, "is that a frame really has a lot more internal structure than just a bunch of slots. There are relationships between the things that fill the slots, and there are things that are true about those relationships that need to be enforced. And we haven't figured out either how to represent those relationships, or how to make them true.

"For example, in the Marriage frame, besides saying the man is a man and the woman is a woman, you also want to make some assumptions about the fact that the woman loves the man and the man loves the woman. If you find out later on that the man doesn't love the woman, you don't want to say that this Marriage frame isn't happening, because that's not a defining feature, it's just a characteristic. But you want to at least notice that this is something unusual and something you should worry about. In

*Shortly after the movie *War Games* came out, the ARPAnet was split into two different networks—R&Dnet, for civilian researchers, and MILnet, a high-security network for military users.

fact, it might suggest the Divorce frame—or, alternatively, the Murder frame, depending on whether you were reading a mystery story or not." He laughed, a high-pitched snort that faded away into a sigh.

"So representing that knowledge and having it actually come into play later on when it's contradicted—we haven't really figured out how to do that yet. And as stories get longer, you're more likely to have things like contradictions happen, or to have a frame fade out of view. If you do a really long story and in the very beginning you hear someone went to a restaurant, and six chapters later you hear that they've gone over to a table, you don't want to say, 'Oh, that's the going-to-a-table-in-the-restaurant script!' There are a lot of hard problems in what we're trying to do, and we're trying to get it to do our simple stories and expand it as our stories get bigger."

So does the system understand anything now? Is frame invocation the same as understanding? Could you say it understands that John loves Mary?

Joe looked uncomfortable. He shifted in his chair. He flexed his jaw muscles. "We would tend to say that, but there are lots of people who would argue that, no, it doesn't understand it. Which is probably true. But if we can take all this and add lots and lots of knowledge to it and have it do more original things, then we'll feel better about it."

He brightened. "One thing that would make it more general would be if any of the different ways to say 'John loves Mary' got translated into the representation that invokes the frame. By putting Yigal's PHRAN program in front of it, you could sit down and say 'John loves Mary' or 'John was in love with Mary' or whatever—all the different things that can get represented in this internal form that causes the frame invocation."

Joe returned to his terminal. He typed in a command and waited for a response. One second . . . two seconds . . . an eternity. Clearly the machine was overloaded. Too many users. Joe leaned back in his chair and sighed. "Well," he said to no one in particular, "I'm afraid the honeymoon with Kim is over."

Yigal's PHRAN program was the natural language "front end" for the planning and understanding programs that Joe and Peter were working on. With PAMELA and PANDORA, everything had to be written out in LISP, in conceptual-dependency form. PHRAN could do that automatically. PHRAN could take ordinary English and convert it into something the computer could process directly. PHRAN was the interpreter.

Language is clearly central to intelligence. It shapes our thoughts, allows us to communicate, makes civilization possible. But despite its role in human intelligence, computer experts weren't always convinced it was important to machine intelligence.

During the Fifties, AI meant logic, puzzles, and games. Natural-language processing was a separate field. It consisted of automatic translation and computational linguistics—useful subjects, but not ones that had much to do with getting computers to think. The people who pursued them were interested in developing tools—mechanical translators, aids to linguistic study.

Early automatic-translation efforts foundered because linguists tried to build systems that translated without any understanding. In theory, these systems would work purely according to the rules of grammar—but in practice, they didn't work at all. They were able to do word-for-word dictionary translations and to formulate technically proper sentences, but translation turned out to be a lot more complicated than that. As a result, what the machines turned out was generally laughable. One oft-repeated example, probably apocryphal but nonetheless emblematic: the English saying "The spirit is willing but the flesh is weak," which reportedly came out in Russian as "The vodka is strong but the meat is rotten."

As failure mounted upon failure, researchers grew sour on the attempt. Anthony Oettinger, who headed a massive Pentagon-funded machine translation effort at Harvard during the Fifties, was so disillusioned he contributed the preface to Dreyfus's book. The Israeli linguist Yehoshua Bar-Hillel worked on the problem for years and finally pronounced it insoluble. In 1966 a blue-ribbon panel set up by the National Academy of Sciences reached the same conclusion. After that, the field quickly died for lack of funding.

Despite the failure of machine translation, a few interesting natural-language processing programs were developed by AI researchers in the Sixties. Daniel Bobrow, a student of Minsky's at

MIT, came up with a program called STUDENT that turned high-school algebra problems into mathematical equations. An MIT professor, Joseph Weizenbaum, developed a system called ELIZA that mimicked the responses of a Rogerian psychotherapist. If you typed in the observation "Men are all alike" (to take an example from Weizenbaum's paper on the subject), it would ask, "In what way?" If you said, "Perhaps I could learn to get along with my mother," it would reply, "Tell me more about your family." Like a nondirective therapist, it would turn anything you said into a question. And if you asked it a question yourself, it would most likely say, "Why do you ask?"

The problem with ELIZA was that there was nothing inside—just a bunch of canned phrases and some rules for forming questions. Aside from those rules, the program didn't know anything about anything. It didn't know about men or mothers, or what a family is, or why anyone would care about these things one way or the other. It was a computational card trick, a programming sleight of hand, and its creator made no claims for its being anything else. But other people did.

Some of them began to talk as if it really could help people. Kenneth Colby, the psychologist Roger Schank worked with at Stanford, wrote a version called DOCTOR and proposed its use as a "therapeutic tool" to help alleviate the shortage of human psychotherapists. When a visiting Soviet scientist sat down at Colby's keyboard, he quickly started pouring out all his troubles, much to the embarrassment of onlookers. He wasn't the only one. Would-be patients besieged Weizenbaum with phone calls, begging him to put them on-line so they could pull themselves together. Weizenbaum got so spooked by all this that he wrote his book, *Computer Power and Human Reason,* in which he condemned AI as the province of madmen and psychopaths. He still labors in the AI lab at MIT, a voice of conscience among the questers, but he is a controversial figure among his colleagues. To them he's an example of what can happen when a scientist becomes obsessed with the social consequences of his research; as one of them put it, "You shouldn't get bogged down because you can't compute the future."

The next significant development in natural language was SHRDLU, a program developed at the end of the decade by

Terry Winograd, then a Ph.D. candidate at MIT. Unlike ELIZA and the computerized translators, SHRDLU knew what it was doing. It wasn't just blindly manipulating symbols; its code contained detailed data structures filled with knowledge about the world and about language. Unfortunately, its particular world was quite small.

Winograd's program could only talk about toy blocks. It could keep track of these blocks in conversation, and it could move them around in its "mind." Within the context of this blocks world, it was remarkably intelligent: It could reason, communicate, understand, even learn (a new shape, for example). But outside the blocks world, it was hopeless.

The problem—and the problem with other limited-domain programs that were built around the same time—was that they were not extensible. SHRDLU had been confined to the blocks world because Winograd felt it would be impossible to program a computer with everything it would need to know about the real world. But maybe—so the thinking went at the time—if programs could be developed to perform in these artificially limited microworlds, they could be extended piecemeal until the whole realm of earthly experience came under their domain. This turned out not to be the case.

The man who pointed this out most vigorously was Roger Schank. While Winograd was building SHRDLU at MIT, Schank was at Stanford developing his conceptual-dependency scheme and building MARGIE, the first of his natural-language systems. For Schank, getting computers to understand natural language was part of the larger problem of getting them to understand— and unlike Winograd, he was prepared to get them to understand everything. It was a bold venture, maybe even crazy, like trying to empty the ocean with a tin cup. And yet for Schank, it was the only way to proceed.

The system PHRAN most closely resembles is ELI, a natural-language program built by Chris Riesbeck, Schank's research associate at Yale. ELI stands for "English Language Interpreter." It was the language module of SAM—Schank's Script-Applier Mechanism. It worked by converting ordinary English sentences into a meaning representation which SAM could then process.

When Wilensky came to Berkeley, he brought ELI with him and gave it to Yigal to study. Yigal started his research by adding things to it. What he added were "pattern-concept pairs"—phrasal patterns paired with meaning representations of the concepts they stand for.

ELI was equipped to deal only with individual words. Faced with a sentence like "John gave Mary a piece of his mind," it would assume that he handed her a piece of something he owned called a "mind." But "piece of my mind" is what's known in linguistics as a "nonproductive" phrase, meaning it can't be produced by following any general rules about language. There are hundreds of these phrases—"the Big Apple," "the Golden Gate" —and they've been causing problems for language-understanding systems for years. Dozens of papers have been written on the problem. Yigal was trying to come up with a solution.

At first he just added phrases to ELI, but he didn't add many before he decided to build a whole new system, not just one that would ride piggyback on Riesbeck's. He called it PHRAN, for PHRasal ANalyzer, and he worked on it for a year and a half. When he finished, he had a system that "understood" some 305 different patterns—170 of them individual words, 135 multiword phrases. It could handle idioms—"kick the bucket," "bury the hatchet." It could handle clichés—"hot as hell," "dressed to kill." It could handle catchphrases—"99 and 44/100 percent pure," "I am not a crook." It didn't know anything about crooks or buckets, but it did know to follow rules about phrases rather than rules about individual words. That meant its data base could be instructed to process "kick the bucket" and "kick the pail" in entirely different ways.

When Yigal presented his first paper on PHRAN, at a meeting in Philadelphia of the Association for Computational Linguistics, he ran into some serious criticism. He claimed it should be able to process phrases in Spanish and Chinese; other people pointed out that it couldn't do that yet. He claimed that a companion system should be able to generate English using the same data base; they pointed out that no such system was in evidence. He claimed that the Schankian approach was useful and valid; they argued that he was wasting his time, that he was making no contribution, that he was tackling the whole problem all wrong.

"People from other groups don't come up to me and say they hate Schank or his group or us or anything," Yigal said, "but one might get that impression just from looking around."

It had been a year and a half now since Yigal had finished his work on PHRAN. In the intervening months, a number of people had added more English-language patterns to the knowledge base, tripling the program's vocabulary. Mike Morgan, a master's candidate from Harvard who later went to Bell Labs, added patterns that enabled it to process sentences in Spanish and Chinese as well as in English. Steve Upstill, another master's candidate, constructed PHRED, a natural-language generating system that uses essentially the same knowledge base. These two programs, mirror images of each other, represented a single solution to the dual problems of language understanding and language generation.

PHRAN still didn't know too much; its vocabulary only took up fifty-six kilobytes of disk-storage space. "You put in a few words, a few phrases, to get it to demonstrate its capabilities," Yigal said. "So if you just come in out of the blue and type a sentence in, the chances are a hundred to one that it will not be able to figure it out. But the point of most of the things we're doing is just to demonstrate that they can be done, and I think I've done that."

Yigal's next task was to look for other problems to solve. PHRAN would have been enough for a master's, but he wanted his Ph.D., and to get it he'd have to solve more than the problem of nonproductive phrases. It took him several months to find another problem; and after he found one, it took him several more months to understand it well enough to start working on it. So it was almost a year after finishing PHRAN that he started work on what has come to be known as the Context Model.

Unlike PHRAN, which only knows about language, the Context Model is designed to know something about the world—not a lot, but enough to carry on an intelligent discussion. It's supposed to be able to keep track of the context of a discussion—to remember what the discussion is about and to know how it's expected to respond.

"I'm trying to capture the notion of focus in a conversation," Yigal explained. "How, if something is continually referred to— not explicitly, necessarily, but implicitly—it remains at the top of what you're dealing with. People have dealt with focus before, but just by saying, 'Okay, this object is in focus, and now *this* object is in focus.' I don't want things to move in and out in such an abrupt way. I'd like to have things lurking in the background."

The Context Model keeps track of things by assigning them different "activation levels." These are numbers, one through ten, that are given to everything in its model of the world. The activation level of any particular item changes every time something new happens. If it's referred to again, its activation level goes up. If the subject is changed, its activation level goes down. Whenever its activation level drops too low, it's automatically moved out of the data base—"forgotten," in a sense.

Forgetfulness, it turns out, is a very good thing. If we didn't forget, we'd remember everything—what we ate last Monday, the names and faces of every one of our first-grade classmates, all the cocktail-party chatter we'd ever heard in our lives. We'd be a mess. In the Context Model, forgetfulness would enable Yigal to deal with the problem of reference—of what certain words refer to in conversation. What do we ever mean by "he" or "she" or "it"? How do we make sense of sentences like "He went to the bank"? Which "he," what bank, and what kind of bank—the kind that handles money or the kind that lies by a river? The Context Model was designed to figure these things out. "That's its way of learning," Yigal said.

"Right now, PHRAN understands sentence by sentence. You say 'John did this' and 'John did that,' and it doesn't even know it's the same John. In fact, it doesn't even know what John is, or what it means for John to do this or that. And it doesn't distinguish a question from anything else. If it's a question, you'd like it to respond. But it just types out a representation that says, 'This is a question,' and that's it. Now I want the system to say, 'Oh, this is a question, so I have to figure out the answer.'

"It doesn't do any sort of generalization, which seems to be a central aspect of learning, because I don't know how to do it. If you drop something on your foot and it hurts and you do it several times, you know that if you drop *anything* heavy on your foot it's going to hurt. But the question is, What can you generalize? When you drop something on one foot and then on the other foot and then on your hand and it hurts, do you generalize that if you drop something heavy on any part of your body it will hurt? You probably do. But it isn't a trivial question. You don't want to generalize about parts of your body all the time—'I can play the piano with my hands, so I can play the piano with my feet.' So it's a problem.

"Another problem is when do you know you don't know how to do something? If there's something the system doesn't know, then it's supposed to call PANDORA, which will figure out how to figure out the answer. But there could be problems, because the more steps you have in the process of figuring out what the answer is, the lower the eventual activation level is going to be. So if there are too many steps in getting the answer, it may forget what it was doing by the time it gets there. I tried to add a little thing that says that if you're asked a question, you should say something eventually. Hopefully, that will make the activation high enough so that it really will say it." He looked dubious.

Like Joe and Peter, Yigal had started out to be a mathematician. He moved to AI because he found math unsatisfying. He couldn't even talk to anybody about it. Somebody would ask him what he did and he'd say, "Oh, I'm in set theory," and that would be the end of the conversation.

Set theory is a branch of mathematics that deals not with numbers but with sets of numbers—or sets of symbols or sets of objects or anything else. You might have the set of all prime numbers, or the set of all x such that $2x = 10$, or the set of all bankers with green hair. This last is what's known as an "empty set"; the first is an example of an "infinite set," because there are an infinite number of prime numbers. Set theory was developed late in the nineteenth century by the German mathematician Georg Cantor. It is full of infinities and riddled with paradox—so much so, in fact, that initially it was shunned as "a disease" and its inventor so hounded by his peers that he died in a mental institution.

We can understand such concepts as the set of all sets, but what are we to make of the set of all sets that do not include themselves as members? Is this set a member of itself, or not? Such conundrums opened up questions about the very foundations of mathematics—questions that culminated in 1931 with Gödel's incompleteness theorem, which showed that in any mathematical system there are statements that cannot be proven according to the rules of that system. (The heart of Gödel's proof was a mathematical rendering of the so-called Gödel sentence, a self-referential paradox that states, "This theorem cannot be proven.") Like Heisenberg's uncertainty principle in physics, Gödel's theorem was something new to science: an acknowledgment that there are fundamental limitations to what we can know.

Yigal's problem with math was that it was too abstract. "At first," he said, "set theory and logic looked promising, because the kind of stuff that was done from the beginning of the century into the Thirties and Forties seemed to pertain to real life. There were questions of what is truth? and things like that. But once you got beyond that, you sort of left the realm of this universe and continued into vast beyonds and infinities of different kinds. No aspect of life had anything to do with it."

The feeling was typical. Artificial intelligence tends to attract the mathematically inclined—the students who love to solve problems. But in college, usually during the undergraduate years, those who go on to become mathematicians seem to sort themselves out from those who go into computer science. The computer students become disillusioned as their problem-solving discipline turns into a realm of infinite abstraction. They cease to understand the problems, or even to be interested in them. Computer science, and AI in particular, offers an alternative: problems that have some grounding in reality. What it lacks is a sense of completeness—a sense that every problem has a solution.

Yigal had spent nearly four years in math before he switched to artificial intelligence. What interested him about AI was natural-language processing. Language was something he'd been thinking about since he was a teen-ager in Israel. How do people express their thoughts? How do other people understand them? Do they understand what was really meant? This was something you could talk about all night. It was a puzzle. Yigal wanted to solve it. The computer offered a means of doing so.

"I view it as sort of a game," he said. "I find getting a machine to understand things entertaining. I'd be very happy if I could find out how people do these things, even if I couldn't program it. But I don't see how you could really know it then. To really know it would be to know it in enough detail that it would be possible to get a machine to do it."

I remarked that language seems so imprecise—so different from math, so alien from computers.

"You have to explain what you mean when you say language is imprecise," Yigal retorted. "Language is precise in its own way. It's produced according to rules, and these rules have to be precise. It's hard to interpret what you hear from someone—in that sense it's imprecise. It isn't that it means imprecise things, it's just that it's hard for us to find out exactly what a person intended it to mean. But I think the person who's producing language is doing it according to some fixed rules that tell him or her what to do. So what I'm doing, essentially, is trying to understand the rules."

Talking with Yigal, I noticed that sometimes he had trouble with my questions. This was especially true of casual, ordinary questions like "What are you working on?" "What am I working on?" Yigal would say, sounding puzzled and a little irritated. "Do you mean *right now,* or what?"

When I asked him about this, he relaxed and gave a short laugh. "I always view these questions as cocktail-party-type questions," he said. " 'Where are you from?' 'What do you do?' People often ask these questions just as a way of starting up a conversation. But if you really want to answer it, it involves so much. It isn't clear what a good answer is going to be.

"But I know how to take care of these things. The perfect icebreaker when somebody asks you 'Where are you from?' is to say, 'What do you mean?' That's enough to start a conversation. They don't know what they mean. They just know they're supposed to ask it, right? And they expect to hear an answer like 'Turkey' or 'Illinois' or something like that."

In Yigal's case, "What do you mean?" would actually be a very reasonable response. He carries two passports—one American, one Israeli. He was born in Manhattan, but when he was an infant his parents moved to Pasadena, and then they moved back east to New Jersey, and when he was six they moved to Israel. They lived in Haifa for a while, and then they moved to a suburb of Tel

Aviv. When he was eighteen, he went to college in Haifa; and after a stint in the army, he went on to Hebrew University in Jerusalem. After that he came to Berkeley.

"Where are you from?" someone might ask. To which Yigal would reply, "What do you mean, where am I from?"

Yigal's father is Moshe Arens, the man who replaced Ariel Sharon as Israel's minister of defense. A Lithuanian-born aeronautical engineer who escaped with his family to America in 1939, Moshe Arens is an airplane designer by training. Politically, he stands far to the right; as a member of the Knesset, he opposed the Israeli-Egyptian peace accord on the grounds that it gave too much away. He served under Menachem Begin in the Irgun Zvai Leumi underground during the first Arab-Israeli war, and thirty-four years later (after receiving engineering degrees from MIT and Caltech) he served under Begin again as the Israeli ambassador to Washington. Asked by a *New York Times* reporter why he'd been picked for the job, he laughed and said, "I speak English."

Yigal's political views are quite different. On the wall above his desk, he'd pasted a decal of the Palestinian flag. "I put it up as a tiny expression of my sympathy with the problems, let's say, or the struggle of the Palestinian people," he said. "Their country is occupied. There are lots of questions about how much of it is really theirs, but no one will argue except some Israelis that the West Bank is not Palestinian. People were kicked out, they are dispersed around the world, they cannot return to what they think is theirs. There's no question about it."

Joe looked up from his terminal at the flag decal. "Is that what that is? I always thought it was some sort of military decoration or something."

Yigal looked at him open-mouthed. "You're kidding! Joe, are you *crazy?*"

Yigal did receive a military decoration for his service in the Israeli Defense Forces. It was a mistake, however, and he certainly didn't have it mounted anywhere. "During my life," he explained, "there have been many errors concerning me by the authorities.

"After they discharged me, it turned out I'd been a sergeant for a long period of time—except I didn't know about it. Nobody knew about it. But that's what it said on all the papers. They even checked with some computer. Another error was that I was given two bachelor's degrees, one in math and one in physics. They mailed them to me. And after I came here I got in the mail a decoration for my contribution to the effort of the 1973 war—which I'd spent in a café in Jerusalem, having been classified as mentally unfit to serve in the military."

As a college student, Yigal had become associated with an anti-Zionist group, the Israeli Socialist Organization. He was also a member of the Academic Reserves, an officer-training outfit, which enabled him to put off military service until he graduated. Eventually someone put these two associations together, and when that happened Yigal received a letter from military intelligence. The letter ordered him to report to an address in Haifa.

When he got there, he found an ordinary apartment building —no sign on the door, no sign on the mailboxes, nothing. He went upstairs. On the top floor, he found a door marked "Military Intelligence." He went in and waited, and finally an officer came out carrying a file with his name on it. The officer started to ask him about his political views.

"My political views?" Yigal said. "Oh, nothing special. Why do you ask?"

The officer wondered if Yigal had thought about how his political views might affect his future. Yigal asked if he was being threatened. "Oh, no!" the officer said. "No, not at all. I was just wondering if you'd thought about it."

Yigal withdrew from the reserves somewhat later, after hearing he might be ordered to infiltrate neighboring Arab countries as part of his training. It wasn't long before he got a notice ordering him to report for duty as a private. After that, peculiar things began to happen.

First he was given a course in communications—but on the day he was supposed to start learning about codes, he was suddenly ordered off the base. He was reassigned to another division and made a clerk at a camp outside Haifa. Then military intelligence discovered he was using the office duplicating machine to run off political material, and he was reassigned yet again. This time he turned up in the branch of the army that forms settlements in the occupied territories. Members of party youth organizations join up as a group and go off to build settlements for their party.

"It could have been bad," he said. "I could have been assigned to some extreme right-wing settlement in the Sinai and just left to *rot* there."

Instead, he was sent to a large basic-training base in the center of Israel. He took advantage of the opportunity to get a psychiatric discharge. He went to a doctor, and the doctor sent him to a psychologist, and the psychologist sent him to the central military hospital. Unfortunately, the people at the military hospital were not very impressed.

"I had a whole story made up on how to get out," he said. "It was worthless. I came back the second time and the doctor said, 'Look, it's not serious. If you want to go to a private psychologist, that's all right. Maybe we can arrange for you to serve next to your home.' When I heard that, I saw my world falling to pieces."

As Yigal was telling me this story the phone rang, and he interrupted himself to answer it. It was Yael, his wife, a poet of some celebrity in Israel. She and Yigal were living in married students' housing in Albany, a suburb in the Berkeley flats—the low-lying area near the bay. He spoke to her in Hebrew for a few minutes, then hung up the phone and resumed his story.

"And then, just as happened here, a phone call came. The doctor had to talk to someone, and I had a couple of minutes to think. When he put the receiver down, I said, 'Look, as long as I'm here, there's this other problem that I neglected to mention before. The problem is that I've taken acid, and ever since then I've had these flashbacks.' Drugs I knew they'd take seriously. 'Oh,' they'd say, 'that's serious. That we have to look into.' That prompted them to send me to a clinical psychologist, and when I came back later they said, 'Okay, we'll have to discharge you.' And I was out in a few days—just in time to start the new school year at Hebrew University."

It was six years later that Yigal joined Wilensky's budding AI group. He'd come to Berkeley with Yael on an exchange program he wasn't exactly eligible for. But the math department granted him a waiver, and the next four years were devoted to set theory.

When he finally decided to switch to AI, his first step was to sign up for two courses. One was Lotfi Zadeh's introductory AI course, where the emphasis was on expert systems, and the other was

113

Wilensky's natural-language course. Joe Faletti was in the natural-language course, too. They didn't know each other at the time, but within a few months they'd be working together.

Things were a bit more informal then: There was no ARPA funding, so researchers weren't paid, and their office, when they finally got it, was a windowless den deep inside the building. Besides Joe and Yigal, the only researchers Wilensky had were master's candidates—mainly Mike Deering, Mike Morgan, and Steve Upstill. Deering worked on PAM, Morgan helped with PHRAN, and Upstill built the natural-language generating program, PHRED.

Just as Steve was about to leave, Paul Jacobs arrived with a master's in applied math from Harvard. He'd been a friend of Mike Morgan's there, and he took over Mike's house in the Berkeley hills and Steve's language-generating program at the same time. PHRED was basically a starter project for him: His job was to make it run faster and more efficiently. When Steve left, it couldn't generate anything in less than four or five minutes. It would have to work a lot faster than that, and its knowledge base would have to be revised to make it fully compatible with PHRAN. Both PHRED and PHRAN, meanwhile, would be continually updated as PAMELA and PANDORA were further developed.

Hooked together, PHRED and PHRAN and PAMELA and PANDORA would theoretically make up a single AI system: language, understanding, goals. "PHRAN is the front end of this whole system," Paul explained. "PHRAN's job is to take English and convert it into a knowledge representation. And in back of this we're going to have this whole understanding system that's gonna have to take input and give output and do most of the work in between. And after it decides what it's going to say, it passes the content to PHRED, and PHRED expresses it.

"So PHRAN is the front end, and PHRED is the back end. PHRED takes a knowledge representation and expresses it as English. And hopefully we can get it to express knowledge in French or Spanish or Italian as well."

That was Paul's next task, as soon as he'd streamlined its English knowledge base—to give it one in Spanish. With a Spanish knowledge base, PHRED would be able to generate sentences in Spanish as well as in English. It was no longer a big problem. At Yale there was already an understanding system that worked in several languages and a generating system that did likewise. Automatic translation, which had seemed such an impossible task two decades before, had fallen before the onslaught of Schankian knowledge-representation schemes. Paul expected to be done by summer.

Dark-haired and tanned, he approached all this with the confident attitude of a Bronx Ivy Leaguer gone California beach boy. "The translation bit," he explained nonchalantly, "is just a side effect of having a good understanding system and a decent parser and a decent generator. We could have had somebody come in and write PHRED in Spanish to start with, and right there we would've had an English-Spanish translator. That might have impressed a lot of people, but doing sentence-by-sentence translation is not really that difficult.

"The knowledge representation that we have is hopefully not language-dependent at all. The language is not important because the knowledge is represented in the computer in some internal form. With a good generator, we can output an idea in any language we want. So the problem of translating is no more complicated than the problem of paraphrasing. It's basically the same thing. It's just: Take this story, convert it into a representation, and spit it back in some language.

"But PHRAN and PHRED are just tools," Paul continued. "The interesting issues are much more global—things like the representation of objects, the description of objects, the description of concepts, the generation of ideas, stuff like that. You know, resolving references—pronoun references and stuff. And how to represent objects—do you want to say 'John 1' for some person x named John? Do you want to say 'the tall man over there'? Those are big issues, but they're not going to be solved by someone who's coming up with a generator. They have to be solved by someone who's working on knowledge representation."

8

Should Robots Have Civil Rights?

I walked into the office the next day to find that the John-loves-Mary story had vanished from the whiteboard. In its place was this:

John was on Cloud 9 (Happy John +9.9)
   Mary had said "Yes"!—Ask = = > All slots invoke?
   Now he needed a tux

Joe and Peter, I discovered, had put the John-loves-Mary story on ice for a while. In its place was a new story. It would give them another test of their frame-invocation mechanism.

"I could try this story on you!" Joe cried as I entered the door. Today he was wearing brown-and-white checked polyester pants and a brown knit shirt with pockets and collar in a matching check. Out the window, the blank gray facade of Davis Hall was dark and swollen with rain. It had been raining for more than a week now. Misty clouds hung low over the hills. Strawberry Creek, the trickling brook that meanders across the campus, had long since become a torrent.

Joe had seen his first snowfall over the weekend on the road to Lake Tahoe. He and his family had been stuck for hours in the Sierra Nevada while a road crew blasted an impending avalanche and then cleared the highway. A foot of snow fell during that time. They didn't have enough gas to go back, and they didn't have enough gas to keep the motor running, so they sat there and got cold. Joe used the opportunity to try the same story on them.

He read the story off the whiteboard, then turned to me with an expectant gleam in his eye. "There are two possible interpretations, we think, and we want to know which one is dominant," he said. "The question is, What does he need a tux for?"

"That's easy," I declared. "He needs a tux for his wedding."

"Darn it!" Joe stamped his foot on the floor and started pacing the room. "That's what almost everyone says—three out of four. My intention was that it be for the senior prom."

"The senior prom? Isn't this the same John and Mary who were just proposing to each other?"

"That's part of the problem," he admitted. "Everybody's been hearing us talking about John and Mary getting married. We just use 'John' and 'Mary' when we mean 'he' and 'she.' And the thing we're working on now is, How is it that you invoke a particular frame? How do you know what frame is appropriate?"

At this point, I countered, the mere mention of John and Mary was enough to start me invoking the Marriage frame.

"See, what we think is, 'John was on cloud nine' just means that John was happy, and there isn't any big chunk of knowledge that you have about that. No frame there. But 'Mary had said "Yes"' ' should at least bring up all you know about asking a question and getting an answer. The problem is that we assume that saying yes must have some connection with John being on cloud nine, but Peter and I don't know how to make that connection."

"What does 'Happy John +9.9' mean?"

"That comes from conceptual dependency," Peter replied. "Schank has these arbitrary scales that go from minus ten to plus ten for all the possible states."

"For some reason," Joe put in, "I decided that cloud nine was only a 9.9 and not a ten."

"I decided it was cloud ten, but—"

"And then there's 'John needed a tux,' " Joe continued. "The question is, Does 'tuxedo' invoke wedding? We decided that any time you need some functional object, you need it for what you normally use it for, which in this case is to dress up in. And the thing you dress up for is a formal occasion. But somehow it's hard

117

to imagine that people have a Formal Occasion frame in their minds." He laughed nervously and shifted to the other foot.

"So we spent this morning looking through conference proceedings to find someone else who's worked on this problem, and essentially they seem to have done either one of two things. Either each frame has in it a specific thing that invokes it—and this seems wrong because there should be lots of ways to invoke the Wedding frame, say—or else everything in the frame has the capability of invoking it. But that's a problem, too, because one of the parts of the restaurant script is someone PTransing to a table, and we don't think that hearing that someone went to a table calls up the restaurant script. So it doesn't seem like it's all of it, and it doesn't seem like it's only one thing. That's where we are at the moment."

Margaret breezed in and announced she'd been studying all day. It was nearly the end of the winter quarter. Exam week was just a couple of days away. Margaret had only two exams, one in computational theory and one in operating systems, but they both fell on Tuesday. Still, she didn't seem unduly concerned. She always managed to look eager and unflappable at the same time; it would take more than a couple of exams to make her sweat.

Joe told her he and Peter were looking for a new story.

"Oh!" she cried. "Why don't you use Anais Nin? She wrote all this pornography! She was in New York in the Forties, and there were all these writers there and they didn't have any money. But there was this rich old man and he paid them a dollar a page to write pornography for him. No plot, just lots of sex."

Joe looked dubious. "I dunno," he said. "It's bad enough we've been doing vasectomy stories lately." Before the marriage story, there had been the vasectomy story: "Mary's husband had a vasectomy. A couple of months later, Mary got pregnant."

But Margaret was bubbling over with ideas. If not Anais Nin, why not Steve Martin? "You could do something from *Cruel Shoes!*" she exclaimed. "Something that makes no sense at all! How about 'The Gift of the Magi Indian Giver'?"

Peter looked at Joe and groaned out loud.

The room next to the AI office was occupied by Ira Pohl, a visiting professor of computer science from UC Santa Cruz who was using his time at Berkeley to lead a graduate-level seminar called "Should Robots Have Civil Rights?" It was a provocative title, he realized, and today he was going to produce the answer. It was right there in the chalkwell in the little classroom in Cory Hall where the seminar had been meeting: a white envelope with the word *Answer* written across it in big red letters.

Pohl's was an unusual seminar. It wasn't really about whether robots should have civil rights. It was about the social impact of AI and robotics. Only three students were taking it, for it was not, strictly speaking, a very practical course. It wouldn't do anything for your programming skills, for example. So most of the people attending turned out to be faculty members.

Pohl himself was a fortyish individual with frizzy black hair and a rampant beard. Though he was slender and bespectacled, all this hair, coupled with his energetic manner and the plaid shirt he wore stuffed with pens, somehow gave him the rough-and-ready appearance of an intellectual lumberjack. He'd studied computer science at Stanford in the Sixties, then worked briefly with the University of Edinburgh's Machine Intelligence Group and at IBM's Watson Research Center in Yorktown Heights, New York, before settling down at Santa Cruz. His research specialties included the esoteric disciplines of search procedure and algorithmic analysis, but in recent years he'd grown increasingly concerned with the transformations computers will wreak on human society.

He'd spent a lot of time on the taxonomy of computer effects —on developing a classification system for the different kinds of changes computer technology will bring. He'd come up with three types of changes. Type one, or methodological effects, are the low-level changes we're beginning to see now: computerized work stations in the office, electronic tellers, and so forth. Type two changes—dislocating effects—are the ones we'll be feeling by the end of the century: the automated office, the robotized factory. This is what will put people out of work: Many observers speculate that by 2000, more than half the manufacturing jobs now held by humans will have been taken over by some sort of "steel-collar worker." And then, in the indeterminate future, there are the type three effects—the ones Pohl sees as paradigmatic.

Paradigm shifts have occurred before. There was a major paradigm shift about 10,000 years ago, when humans first began to abandon the hunter/gatherer life-style in favor of agriculture. There were multiple paradigm shifts from the seventeenth to the nineteenth centuries, when the Scientific Revolution and the Industrial Revolution transformed a feudal, agrarian society into a mass industrial society. During that period, as new discoveries were made and new inventions exploited, humans found their view of themselves and their place in the world repeatedly rearranged. Before the end of this century, Pohl contends, computers will cause this to happen all over again.

He's not alone in this belief. In *Megatrends*, for example, John Naisbitt predicts the death of representative democracy and bureaucratic hierarchies. In *The Third Wave*, Alvin Toffler predicts the simultaneous demise of the nation-state, of mass industrial society (mass production, mass marketing, mass media, mass consumption . . .), and of what we now call work. As radical as such changes seem, there's no turning away from them, for twentieth-century advances in science and technology have put mankind at the window. Outside lies either nuclear annihilation or an entirely new world, a world that will be as different from what we know now as ours is from the Middle Ages. And yet, as the National Research Council—an arm of the National Academy of Sciences—drily remarked in a five-year *Outlook for Science and Technology*, "Public discussion has not begun to reflect this perspective in any adequate way." Pohl's seminar was a modest attempt at redress.

But before he gave the Answer, there would be a presentation by Bartlett Mel, the only undergraduate in the seminar. A baby-faced young man whose father teaches biophysics at Berkeley, Mel was an electrical engineering/computer science major who'd recently developed an interest in AI. Curly-haired and blond, he looked a bit like Gene Wilder in the classroom scene that opens *Young Frankenstein*. His paper was on the nature of understanding in humans and computers.

He began by quoting a statement that's often bandied about by AI researchers, the contention that "humans and computers are two species in the genus of information-processing systems." It was not an idea that appealed to him. To refute it, he tried to draw a distinction between two types of knowledge—"machine-dependent" and "machine-independent." The latter he described as knowledge that can be written down and that can, as a result, be understood by humans and computers alike. Machine-dependent knowledge would be everything that's left—stuff no computer could comprehend because no computer shares our feelings, our daily experiences, our physical bodies. It was, Mel admitted, an intuitive position.

Peter Norvig was in the room, and arguments like this made him itchy. "You've said a lot of vague things," Peter declared at one point, "but the vaguest is your distinction between machine-independent and human knowledge. I think it comes down to the things you know how to express. I don't think it's qualitatively any more difficult to express love than to express a chair."

Actually, it's not all that easy to express a chair. How, exactly, do you know a chair when you see one, and where do you draw the line between a chair and a stool? This was the kind of thing philosophers and psychologists and AI people could argue about for decades. On the other hand, Joe and Peter had the Love frame pretty much set up.

But Pohl was impatient. He had the Answer. "Is the envelope sealed?" someone inquired. "Yes, the envelope is sealed," Pohl replied. He pulled a movie screen down over the blackboard and switched on a projector next to his desk. The screen lit up with a cartoon of a man standing in front of a computer terminal. "We know all about you," said the writing on the terminal screen. "Everything."

"We are about to unleash a social revolution," Pohl declared. He held up the latest issue of *Business Week*. It was opened to an article on artificial intelligence. The article told about the advent of "computerized consultants" in fields such as medicine, geology, and microchip design. It told about the development of computers that can talk and robots that have artificial senses—vision, hearing, touch. It listed some of the researchers who've gone into business: Edward Feigenbaum of Stanford (Teknowledge, Intelli-Genetics); Charles Rosen, formerly of SRI (Machine Intelligence Corporation); Larry Harris, formerly of Dartmouth (Artificial Intelligence Corporation); Roger Schank of Yale (Cognitive Systems). "All this gives me tremendous pause," Pohl declared. "Are we really thinking about where we're going when the people who are preparing to get us there are being bought up and plunged into it before *they* know where we're going?"

Then there was the issue of "AI unemployment"—the prospect of computers and robots taking over jobs. Raj Reddy, the head of the robotics lab at Carnegie-Mellon, reported that more than 25 million Americans are currently employed in manufacturing; he expects that number to drop to 3 million by 2010. And we can't expect the slack to be taken up by service jobs and white-collar work, he added, because computers will be taking over those jobs as well. Then he observed that no one—no one in government, no one in business, no one in power—understands what's happening.

Pohl waited a moment for that to sink in. Then he read the final paragraph, in which the *Business Week* reporter breezily declared, "Over the long run, though, Reddy is certain that disaster will be avoided—somehow." Pohl put down the magazine and stared openmouthed at the classroom. "This guy's at the head of this thing," he said, "and he thinks *everything will be okay somehow?*" He paused, shook his head, and reached for the envelope in the chalkwell.

"It's not sealed," someone cried out.

"No," Pohl admitted. "But it's *capable* of being sealed." He reached inside and pulled out a sheet of paper. It had two answers written on it. He read the first answer:

"Yes, if they can feel pain."

There was a stir in the room. Pohl said there was another possible answer that was related to a fundamental law of computability. He read the second answer:

"There are questions without answers."

The stir began to grow into a general air of disgruntlement. "Some of you may not like that answer," Pohl observed. He reached into the envelope again and pulled out another envelope. This envelope was labeled "The Real Question."

He opened the second envelope and pulled out a second slip of paper. Once again he read aloud:

"Should we build machines that raise such questions?"

General pandemonium ensued. As I edged out the door, I heard Pohl arguing with a visiting professor from Penn State—a specialist in computational complexity, I later discovered—about the futility of even asking such questions. "You can't stop what's already happening," the visitor was saying. "That's true," Pohl replied, "but it's still not too late to have some influence."

"Should robots have civil rights?" Yigal looked dubious. "Well, right. I suppose most people debate this question, right? I feel that it hinges on whether this thing is a sentient, feeling being—as opposed to a car. Should a car have civil rights? It's a really tough question."

I'd walked into the office to find Yigal playing Rubik's Cube on Kim. Graphically, Kim was a bit limited—no color displays, for example—but with the Rubik's Cube program, you could make do. Different letters stood for the different colors on the cube; rows of letters could be rotated by punching keys; and the whole thing was splayed out on the terminal screen like so:

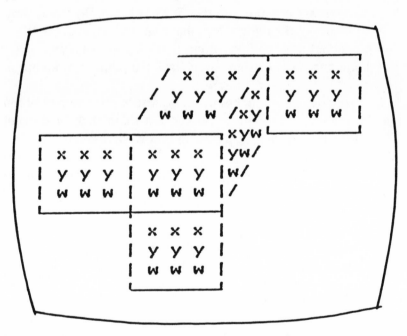

"People train gorillas to talk in sign language," Yigal declared. "Do they deserve civil rights, too? Should they be considered stupid people or something, or are they different because they're gorillas? I don't know. It's a very good question.

"To my mind, the question of whether or not something is a real human being seems to depend a lot on whether it has its own volition. The question will be relatively simple as long as people are still putting these things together. If you have robots producing robots on their own, then in people's minds it may become a more important question. This, however, does seem to be in the relatively distant future." He smiled thinly. "You could also ask, 'What are we going to do if the earth is going to burn because the sun is exploding and there isn't enough room on the rocket ships for everybody?' "

"Well, yes," I replied, "except that nobody in this room is trying to nudge the earth any closer to the sun."

Yigal shrugged. "I'm sure it's a toughie," he said. "It's hard for me to even imagine a scenario where you have robots walking around that you treat as you would human or almost-human beings. I suppose most of the people here, including myself, believe in principle that it is possible. But it's hard to really understand the implications of having things like that walking around. When you talk about a humanlike robot, that's about as far from what I'm doing here as it is from this chair." He pointed to an empty chair.

"It also, of course, touches on the question of whether *people* should enjoy human rights. A robot is a thing that I construct. What does it mean that I constructed it? Well, it means I can run in and change the program so that it doesn't *want* human rights, or I can *train* it so that it doesn't want human rights. But if you can do that to a group of people, does that mean they don't deserve them either?"

Should people have civil rights? A worldwide consensus has never been reached. Should computers decide the question? They may do so by default.

They won't even need intelligence to do it. The proliferation of public and private data banks has created an electronic window on the lives of everyone who uses a credit card, keeps a bank account, applies for insurance, files a tax return, or has a telephone. AT&T, TRW, the IRS, the DoD, the CIA, the FBI—these organizations and dozens more maintain vast data banks filled with extremely detailed information, accurate and otherwise, about the lives and habits of millions of humans. Whom you called and for how long; how much money you made and how you spent it; where you traveled and what hotels you stayed in; what cars you rented and where you drove them; what magazines you receive and what causes you support; where you ate dinner last month or ten years ago—all this is available to anyone, authorized or not, who has the proper passwords.

It was always impractical to keep this much data on paper, but computer technology has made it possible to store it all on spools of magnetic tape. Most of these tapes are the property of powerful institutions—government, banks, corporations, the military. With the passage of time, the computers that read them have grown more and more capable of communicating with one another. Barriers exist, but they are paper restrictions and of little use against the momentum of electronic data flow.

The Privacy Act of 1974 prohibits U.S. government agencies from sharing information with each other or with outside organizations without written permission from the individual involved. Yet in 1977, the Carter administration proudly announced a plan to match computer files on federal employees against lists of welfare recipients to make sure no bureaucrats were getting illegal benefits on the side. Few people objected when computers were used against bureaucratic welfare chiselers, so the Reagan administration came up with a plan to use IRS data to help the Selective Service find teen-agers who fail to register for the draft, and to help the Social Security Administration catch oldsters who fail to report the interest they receive on their bank accounts— even though such information is supposed to be collected for tax purposes only.

How long, you might ask, before the computerized files of the IRS are turned against political dissidents? That happened during the riot years of the Sixties. When black ghettos were set aflame in Oakland, Los Angeles, Chicago, and Washington, the Justice Department set up a special computer network known as the Interdivision Information Unit to keep track of suspected instigators. Later the target group was expanded to include antiwar protesters and New Left activists, and data provided by military intelligence units were collected by the IDIU and turned over to the IRS so that audits could be performed on selected individuals. Within the IRS, a secret Special Service Group was created to look into the tax-exempt status of "dissident" organizations ranging from the John Birch Society to the Legal Aid Society to *Playboy* magazine to—curiously enough—the government's own Civil Rights Commission.

Meanwhile, the CIA was setting up Operation Chaos, a computerized effort to ferret out links between the American peace movement and Communist powers. No such links were ever found, but Operation Chaos went on regardless; at one point, more than 300,000 citizens were profiled in its data banks. The program was illegal, since the CIA's charter explicitly prohibits it from engaging in domestic operations, but that kind of technicality was easily ignored.

One of the most powerful arms of the government is the publicity-shy organization known as the National Security Agency. Headquartered at an army base near Washington, the NSA has a budget reported to be twice as big as the CIA's (the exact amount is classified) and an electronic listening network that circles the planet. Its mission is twofold: to penetrate and monitor the worldwide communications grid—the invisible data net that is the pulse of the information age—while at the same time ensuring that the Pentagon's own communications links are secure. Secretly established by executive fiat in 1952, it operates without Congressional charter and hence without even theoretical limits on its powers.

From the beginning, the NSA has engaged in questionable activities. For twenty-odd years, with the cooperation of ITT, RCA, and Western Union, it routinely and illegally monitored telegrams entering and leaving the country. During the Vietnam period, it also monitored the international telephone calls of people who'd been placed on a government "watch list" because of their political activities. Both programs, code-named Operation Shamrock and Operation Minaret respectively, were suddenly halted when the Senate's Select Committee on Intelligence began investigating in the post-Watergate years. What, if anything, took their place is a question almost no one outside the agency can answer. But if, as committee chairman Frank Church once observed, the agency ever decided to turn the full force of its apparatus against the domestic communications network, "there would be no place to hide."

Just as computers have led to an exponential growth in the information available, intelligent computers will lead to an exponential growth in its usefulness. Natural-language systems, for example, should make it possible for an organization not just to store and retrieve vast amounts of data but to use that data automatically. The IPP program at Yale has already demonstrated the feasibility of feeding newspaper stories or embassy reports or police dossiers into a computer and getting out interesting conclusions about the behavior of terrorists, say, or organized-crime figures, or people who give money to the wrong causes. And then there's the whole area of speech-understanding systems, which do language understanding and speech recognition as well.

We were in the AI office, talking about the possible abuses of artificial intelligence. "I guess the classic example in natural language," Marc was saying in a matter-of-fact tone, "is when you build a system that understands language and then you build a system that understands speech. And then you just tap every phone line."

"That's something that can't be done today, simply because of manpower limitations," Yigal put in. "You need a person to listen to everything. But if you could get an automatic system to, not necessarily *understand* everything, but at least weed out those things that are clearly of no interest, I'm sure that would make some people very happy."

In fact, research has been funded that might make such things possible. In 1971, ARPA announced a five-year plan to produce speech-understanding systems capable of understanding American English from a number of different speakers. Their primary limitations would be in vocabulary and syntax: You could talk to them abut data retrieval, say, but not about the weather. Five years and $15 million later, four systems had been produced—one at SRI, two at Carnegie-Mellon, and one at the Cambridge research-and-development firm of Bolt Beranek & Newman. The most successful of them, Carnegie-Mellon's HARPY, succeeded in understanding 184 sentences from three men and two women with a 5-percent error rate.

When ARPA officials were asked at a meeting what they wanted to do with such a device, they said the military wanted to be able to control its ships, planes, and weapons by voice command rather than by hand control. Certainly there's an understandable appeal to the idea of being able to tell your submarine when to dive, or to communicate with your space station the way Keir Dullea did with HAL in *2001*. If the ARPA project is a valid indicator, however, we're still a bit removed from the intelligent listening device or the animated battle station. Most experts believe it will be well into the next century before humans will be able to talk with computers the way they talk with other humans.

But less dramatic capabilities are not so far off. IBM is working on a system that will take dictation; MIT is developing one that will identify words spoken by different people; Intel is developing a special chip to make such tasks easier; and the researchers in Japan's Fifth Generation computer project have set speech recognition as one of their major goals. Moreover, *New York Times* reporter David Burnham, in his book *The Rise of the Computer State*, reports that there are recurring rumors that the NSA has secretly developed a system that scans tape recordings of international phone calls and automatically flags any call in which certain trigger words turn up—*plutonium*, for example, or *Cuba*. Because of the wall of silence that surrounds everything NSA does, Burnham writes, "determining whether the agency actually has developed such an ability simply is not possible."

With or without the capacity for speech recognition, however, machine intelligence has a lot of appeal to the military. A 1981 report to the Defense Science Board put AI seventh in a ranking of "order-of-magnitude" defense technologies for the 1990s. (Other technologies included high-speed supercomputers, very high-speed integrated circuits, radiation-hardened electronics, space-based nuclear weapons, and antipersonnel microwave generators.) The report noted that AI would be particularly useful in crisis management, in autonomous weapons such as cruise missiles and torpedoes, and in expert data bases for use in "high-stress environments." It recommended that funding be increased from

$13 million annually to $25 million, with more focus on applications and less on basic research.

"I dunno," Marc said, leaning back in his chair and pulling on his yarmulke. "It's difficult, you know? I would never consider going into the American army or working for the army outright. And ARPA may say this is what they're interested in, but maybe they want to build these little robot men to go inside Russia or something. Here we are talking about restaurants and things, but I guess eventually somebody will be able to take that research and build a system that actually—"

"It's a complicated problem," said Yigal. "I'd hate to know that bugging phones is what my system is being used for. Who knows? I think it's a bit far from being practical. The problem exists in almost anything. You can probably use this a lot more outside the military than you can in, and almost everything can be used inside the military, so it's more a question of balance. One day, if I design something that I think can be used for terrible things, then maybe that'll be the day to decide maybe I shouldn't pursue it."

"It's a problem with all of science," Marc declared. "I think the field it's the biggest problem with is physics. I don't think working in AI is any worse than any other field in engineering or computer science—probably less so.

"One of the things I say to myself is that a lot of what I'm really interested in, particularly in natural language, is not only in building a system that works but in finding something out about how people solve the same problems. I think that's an important thing. And I don't have the view that research is directed a certain way because of the funding. They're interested in various things, but mostly they want the field to sort of expand and see what happens. When you write your thesis, they want a copy of it because they paid for the research, but I'm sure they just file it away somewhere."

Outside, the rain had stopped. White clouds drifted lazily across a dazzling blue sky. Wilensky popped into the office to say that he'd just sent something to Schank on the ARPAnet and Schank had written back furious: "How dare you send me mail from California when we're having a blizzard here?"

Marc had his theory exam tomorrow. He started pulling papers out of his knapsack and piling them on his desk. There were dozens of them—notes, reports, Xerox copies, all wadded up and bundled together. Marc was not the neatest of individuals. On his midterm he'd been penalized for his handwriting. Once he didn't get a grade at all because the teaching assistant couldn't read his name. He gathered all the papers in a heap and started shuffling through them. It would be half an hour before he was done.

The day was over now. Students were going home—30,000 of them, each one pursuing some esoteric branch of knowledge that presumably would lead to a place in the world. Quantum electronics . . . symbolic manipulation . . . optimization theory . . . macroeconomics . . . Buddhist studies . . . engineering geoscience . . . Mesopotamian archaeology . . . mass spectroscopy . . . interplanetary studies . . . differential psychology . . . insect nematology . . . wood science . . . bioenergetics: Not a branch of human knowledge went unrepresented. As the students spilled out into the late-afternoon sun, the shimmering bells of the Campanile cast a spell over all, as if to bathe scholarship in a crystalline glow.

At the edge of the campus, in a grove of towering eucalyptus trees, a gathering had formed in a circle of stumps. Forty people, most of them young and black, were beating congas and cowbells and sticks and gourds around a smoldering campfire. "People's liberation" posters were tacked to the trees. A bearded man in a blue knit cap played conga drums and shouted and rolled his head. A man with a clarinet made intermittent squawks. It was dark in the grove. The ground was thick with peeling bark, the air was densely fragrant. A handful of students looked on, pale in the filtered light, transfixed by the throbbing rhythms. The bells of the Campanile were inaudible here.

A few yards farther on, at the other end of the grove, the drums were inaudible, too. Some birds chirped gaily in the trees, and then there was nothing but the roar of city traffic as it skirted the collegiate preserve.

9

A Fork in the Ground

"Lunch-p?"

Wilensky tapped lightly at Zadeh's office door. Inside was a rabbit warren lined with paper: floor-to-ceiling bookcases jammed with books and journals, stacks of plastic baskets stuffed with papers, filing cabinets overflowing with more papers, a magazine rack crammed with more journals. A narrow path led to Zadeh's desk, barely visible beneath its load. An aluminum stepladder dangled from the ceiling.

In hacker slang, the suffix -p? is used to make a question. Zadeh grinned at the invitation. A small man, thin and almost bald but for some wispy strands of hair curling over his collar, he had the narrow eyes and extravagant clothes of a South American gambler. In fact he's an Iranian mathematician turned American computer theorist, a radical logician with an animated expression and an eagerly solicitous smile.

Zadeh has long been a fixture of the AI community, not as a practitioner but as a critic—a friendly critic, unlike Dreyfus and Searle. His own contribution to computing was the invention of fuzzy logic. In 1965, he published a landmark paper entitled "Fuzzy Sets" in which he proposed a means of mathematically accommodating imprecise concepts like height or beauty. Does a fellow who's 5'11" belong to the set of tall men? Using fuzzy logic, he might be declared a partial member. He could be assigned a degree of membership somewhere between 0 and 1, where 1 denotes membership and 0 denotes exclusion. Such notions are heresy to classical logicians, since they violate Aristotle's law of the excluded middle—the rule that says you can't be x and not x at the same time. This kind of black-and-white, either/or reasoning lies at the core of Western thought, which perhaps explains why fuzzy math is more accepted in places like China and Japan than in the United States—and why Zadeh is regarded by some as a dangerous man.

Wilensky and Zadeh chatted amiably as they ambled across the campus to the Golden Bear. They walked under the shadow of the Campanile, past the ivy-covered facade of old South Hall, past the Beaux Arts grandeur of Wheeler, through the wide arch of Sather Gate, and out into Sproul Plaza. It was a five-minute journey that took them from order to the edge of anarchy. Though it's the center of student life at Berkeley, Sproul Plaza is seldom visited by anyone from the engineering school—ostensibly because it's on the other side of campus, but really because the freewheeling sensibility of the place is so alien to the engineering mind.

It was here that the Free Speech Movement had begun some two decades before—in the fall of 1964, just a few weeks before the Big Game with Stanford, when an ex-student was arrested for running a civil-rights recruitment table in violation of campus rules. It happened at noon, when the plaza—a slab of asphalt at the foot of Telegraph Avenue, with the Student Union on one side and the Administration Building on the other—was jammed with people. Student political involvement was already a hot issue; this time it boiled over. The squad car that was sent to take the prisoner away was itself held prisoner for nearly a day and a half. For weeks afterward, students held daily rallies in the plaza to demand free speech. The board of regents finally relented after John Baez led a sit-in at the Administration Building that ended in more than 700 arrests. The Free Speech Movement ended then, but the student activism it sparked had just begun.

That activism is now mostly a memory. A couple of months earlier, a nationwide poll of college freshmen had revealed what most people already knew: American students were drifting to the right. More of them were interested in achieving financial security than in developing a meaningful philosophy of life; and for the first time since the poll began in 1966, more of them identified themselves as conservatives than as liberals. At Berkeley, only 15 percent had taken part in a campus demonstration. Fraternities and sororities were back, and button-down shirts and Weejuns had replaced tie-dyes and combat boots.

But in Sproul Plaza, the past mingled helter-skelter with the present. A thirtyish man with a long brown ponytail sat on the steps of the Student Union, strumming a guitar and crooning Dylan songs—"Blowin' in the Wind," "Don't Think Twice, It's All Right." A student zipped past on a unicycle. A man in a red T-shirt hawked books from a red stand: *The Manifesto of the Communist Party, From Genesis to Genocide, A History of the Guyanese Working People 1881–1905.* Teams of clean-cut young men hurled water-filled prophylactics through the air in celebration of National Condom Week. A phalanx of smoothie wagons dispensed fruit shakes at the outside perimeter.

Zadeh and Wilensky ducked into the cafeteria. Wilensky opted for the Calcutta Chicken—"Black Hole Curry," he called it—and together they took an elevator to a faculty dining room upstairs. Though plainly furnished, it was a room that seemed suspended in air: high-ceilinged and luminous, with vast plate-glass window walls looking out into the treetops above Strawberry Creek. The chaos of Sproul Plaza was just a few yards away, but this was a world removed.

Arrayed around a group of Formica-topped tables in the middle of the room were a dozen of America's more distinguished cognitive scientists: John Gumperz, a roly-poly anthropologist with Einstein hair and a special interest in the sociolinguistics of speech-act theory; Dan Slobin, a bearded psycholinguist in a denim shirt; Eleanor Rosch, a soft-spoken psychologist well known for her ground-breaking work on the nature of concepts and categories; Charles Fillmore, one of the leading critics of Chomskyan linguistics; Hubert Dreyfus, still adamant in his anticognitivism. Gumperz was being asked about an Australian linguist who was going to be at Berkeley for the summer—a man who'd studied a primitive New Guinean tribe known as the Yimas and come back with the news that their language has only ninety verb stems. People were skeptical. Ninety verb stems? What could you say with ninety verb stems? And how did he *know* they had only ninety verb stems? He lived with them for a year, Gumperz said. Wilensky gave a wry smile. "You could do that in California and you'd probably think there were something like six words," he said. "You could get by with 'really' and 'far out' and . . . "

The Yimas, it appeared, were equally limited. But they were a small tribe and the members all knew each other, which doubtless made things easier. Also, certain concepts were simply alien to their experience. You couldn't say "she wanted him to leave but she didn't say anything," for example, because no Yimas would ever fail to say anything like that. You could only say "she told him to leave"—but you couldn't say that either, because there's no indirect quotation in Yimas, and only a single verb to describe speech acts.

"What's the speech-act verb?"

"To say."

A hush fell across the room. People shook their heads and exhaled slowly.

"That's incredible."

"No! I don't believe it."

Gumperz was at a loss to explain the Australian's findings. "I think what he was trying to say," he said, "is that it's a system of communication that only works in this small group, by virtue of the shared knowledge that the small group has. But he got all hung up trying to explain this theory of clause linkages, and I don't think he really argued his case."

"It's not to be believed," Wilensky declared, looking up from his curry. "What happens when the anthropologist comes and this guy goes running back to the village—he can't tell anybody about it because—"

"Bill's not an anthropologist," Gumperz put in. "Bill's a linguist."

"Oh, I see. So he would have gotten the story wrong."

"I think he understands this language much better than he was able to tell us," another professor remarked.

"That's a problem with English," Wilensky quipped. "In English it's considered improper to talk about these things. In Yimas it's probably very easy."

"Someday we should have a seminar on the expressive potential of systems that have very restricted vocabularies, like this language he works with, the basic English used in pidgin, the mother-in-law languages—"

"What languages?"

"Australian aborigine languages, which have this separate language for talking to certain taboo relatives. They have a greatly reduced vocabulary for them, and they have to paraphrase everything using this reduced vocabulary."

The only person in the room who'd actually studied a New Guinean tribe was Eleanor Rosch, so when she offered a comment on the mother-in-law languages, everyone was naturally attentive. "This sounds like the kind of thing that parents do when they want to talk in front of their children and not be understood, but they don't have a foreign language," she said. "They might want to talk about taking the kid to a doctor, and so they'd do that kind of thing." She gave a little cough and smiled sweetly. "Maybe that was the language they used when anthropologists came."

The room exploded into laughter. After a few seconds, however, the burst of guffaws dissolved into a tense and painful silence. "Oh, God," the man beside me cried. "What if that's true?"

As a nice Jewish boy from Brooklyn, Wilensky knew firsthand the ways of tribes. "Have you read *Portnoy's Complaint?*" he asked me one afternoon. "I grew up in that family. My mother was the dominant presence. She wrote the rules, and the rules were the rules that she learned in the *shtetl* when she was growing up. They didn't make sense anymore, but that didn't affect the way I was raised a whole lot."

Wilensky was brought up in a strictly Orthodox family—Orthodox, uneducated, and poor. They lived in a close-knit community in East New York until he was eleven, when an influx of blacks precipitated a Diaspora to the faraway lands of Coney Island, Flatbush, and Sheepshead Bay. Wilensky's family settled in the remotest of them all—Sheepshead Bay, in a little apartment on Avenue Z. Though densely urban, East New York had been a real neighborhood, the *shtetl* transplanted in America. Sheepshead Bay was a leap into the supermarket age.

Bob shared a bedroom with his sister, Sandra, until he went

away to college. She was the one who made good. She grew up, became a doctor, and married a doctor. Bob was the rebellious one. His father still thinks he wasted his college education: He became the wrong kind of doctor.

"Since I was very young, I knew something was wrong," Wilensky told me. "It took a little time to realize what it was. But you know, my feeling is that Jews are really Zulus who happen to live in New York City. *Zulus!* I mean, they have these *weird* rituals! You're brought up in this culture where they have all these rules that are hundreds of years old, were developed in the Middle Ages or whatever, and there are all these conflicts between these rules and the fact that you're living in a culture of poverty.

"You're familiar with all this business that you're supposed to have two sets of dishes and two sets of silverware—one for meat and one for dairy? Now, suppose you contaminate a fork. If you're rich, maybe you'd throw it out and buy a new fork. But a fork was a big deal because you had *a* fork, and you weren't about to throw it out. So what do you do with your contaminated fork?

"Well, the culture has to evolve some way of purifying these things, so you have purification rituals. Don't ask me why, but the purification ritual among this tribe was that you bury the fork in the ground for three days and at the end of that time it becomes purified. The earth cleanses it. But here's the rub. We're in New York City! *Where are you gonna get the dirt to bury the fork?*

"Now, it used to be in Europe that this was fine, your floors were dirt, you could bury it right inside the house. But here you are in New York, you're living in an apartment in Brooklyn, what are you gonna do? When I was growing up, there was always a fork growing next to the dieffenbachia or whatever it was. There was some plant, and it had a fork buried in it! This was a common thing!

"A big issue—a *big issue*—is that you're not allowed to turn the light on or off during the sabbath. But what about going to the bathroom in the middle of the night? So you have to leave the bathroom light on. But then you might shut it off by accident, and that's also a sin. So what you do is you put a piece of tape over the light switch, so when you touch the tape you'll feel it and stop.

"Another thing is, here you are, it's Friday night, you can't go out or have any fun from sunset on, you're sitting in the house with absolutely nothing to do, and here is the most powerful force of the twentieth century sitting in the middle of the living room —your television set. But you can't turn it on. So what do you do? It's a very serious problem.

"What you do is, you buy one of these timers and you set it. You take this thing and you set it to go on for the nine o'clock movie and to go off after the news. So you're sitting there and and you're not doing anything and all of a sudden, *click!* You say, 'Oh, look at that! A television! It happens to be on! *I* didn't do it!' Until I was thirty years old, I thought those timers were for turning on your television set on Friday night. I had no idea they were for lights or burglars.

"These were the kinds of things I was growing up with, and it was obvious to me that I did not wanna live my life according to these rules, okay? It was crazy, and I didn't believe any of it anyway. I had a certain respect for it, but I knew the only way to survive was to leave. There was no question in my mind that it was a matter of sanity."

It was 1968 when Wilensky left Brooklyn, after a summer spent proofreading the Manhattan telephone directory. He spent the next ten years in New Haven, first as an undergraduate at Yale, then as a computer programmer at Yale Medical School, and finally as a grad student in AI. He experienced an exhilarating feeling of liberation. He never looked back.

Yale at the time was a world of privilege under siege. What had begun in the early 1700s as a bastion of learning in the wilderness had developed, some two-and-a-half centuries later, into a training ground for the Protestant elite. History, literature, and the classics were the preferred areas of study; crew and lacrosse the most popular sports. But New Haven, which had been founded as a Puritan theocracy, had become the seventh-poorest city in the United States. By 1968, the invisible borders that protected the sons of Eli from the world around them were being breached willy-nilly. Black Panthers were occupying the campus. Women turned up in the freshman class. Jews were all over the place. A lot of alumni were upset.

Much of this was lost on Wilensky; after all, he was Jewish, and it was the first time he'd been outside New York City. To him,

Yale was all blue blazers and blond hair. He didn't even know what was English and what was Yiddish. When his roommate announced that he was hungry, Wilensky said, "Yeah, I feel like a nosh myself." "A nosh?" came the puzzled reply. "What's a nosh?" And so on.

As freshmen, Yale students join one of a dozen residential colleges, each with its own master, dean, library, dining hall, sports teams, drama clubs, and unique personality. These colleges were created in the thirties during a fit of academic nostalgia; the English magazine *Punch* once described them as "a stage set made in Hollywood for a musical about Oxford." Wilensky was assigned to Silliman, an ivy-covered block of Georgian brick mixed with Tudor stone. The walls of Silliman are dotted with plaques: Here stood the barn where in 1639 the members of the New Haven Colony met to worship and to organize a government; here stood the house of Noah Webster, class of 1778; here stood the old Sheffield Scientific School, precursor of Yale's engineering school. And it was here, behind high iron fences and securely locked gates, that Wilensky made his acquaintance with the world beyond Brooklyn.

One of the distinguishing characteristics of Silliman is its large rooms. Wilensky had three roommates, and together they made up a miniature UN: There was a WASP, a Catholic, an Arab, and himself. The Arab was his best friend, a Pakistani named Pasha whose father was the economic adviser to the king of Saudi Arabia; they called him "Wog." The WASP was a jock who seemed to be good at anything he picked up; his name was Jeff. Billy was the Catholic, a football player from Cleveland who quit his position as a starting lineman so he could express himself through modern dance.

The gates of Silliman open out onto Hillhouse Avenue, a short, leafy street lined with nineteenth-century mansions interspersed with twentieth-century classroom buildings: mathematics, statistics, psychology, engineering. This was the world Wilensky discovered next. He'd always been inclined toward math and science, and for a person of his background—someone who lacks the polish you acquire at Andover or Exeter—it was the preferred way to go.

He had a problem with science, however: He didn't like working in the lab. "I was hung up on this thing that I was too smart to be pushing test tubes around," he explained with a grin. "I still feel that way." So he majored in math, which he found easy. He took only one course in computer science, and that was a nightmare: The department was just getting set up, no one knew how the system worked, files were constantly disappearing, the whole experience was a waste. And yet after graduation he ended up taking a programming job at Yale Medical School. He'd played with computers in high school, he knew FORTRAN, he'd done some programming in machine language and assembly language, and he told them he knew more than he did. He figured anything he needed he could pick up.

Soon he was an addict, a confirmed hacker. He hacked everything in sight—and then he decided, for reasons he couldn't quite articulate, to go to grad school in computer science. He was kind of interested in theory—in numerical analysis, maybe—but on his first day as a grad student, he followed a friend into Roger Schank's natural-language course. He wasn't quite sure what "natural-language processing" meant, but it sounded interesting. Then Schank walked into the room. All of a sudden it was *Bam! Excitement! Talk!* And then, an hour later, it was all over. Wilensky was hooked.

Schank had just arrived at Yale himself. There were maybe fifteen people in this first class; five of them ended up getting Ph.D.'s in AI. Most of them he put to work on SAM, the Script-Applier Mechanism, a big, sprawling project headed by an engineering student named Rich Cullingford. But SAM was basically a straightforward application of script theory, which Schank had developed at a Swiss research institute before coming to Yale. He had a more speculative project in mind as well—PAM, the Plan-Applier Mechanism, the theory for which was much less complete. SAM was an organizational problem, PAM much more a conceptual problem. It seemed to call for a solo approach, someone who wouldn't want to be told what to do.

At the end of the semester, Wilensky went to see Schank in his office. He told him he wanted to do AI. Schank looked surprised. "Oh," he said, "I thought you were going to do something in theory." Then he reached into his desk and pulled out a tiny notebook. Wilensky saw a list of names inside, and next to his was the word *PAM.* "Oh," he said, "what's that?" Four years later, he found out.

Wilensky remained a hacker throughout his grad-student years. He also became a fan of "The George Burns and Gracie Allen Show"—"partly from an AI point of view," I was told by Chris Riesbeck, Schank's research associate. Wilensky came into Riesbeck's office one day and said he didn't understand how people who didn't study AI could understand Burns and Allen, because so many of the things that Gracie got wrong were pronominal references. Given a choice of two different meanings of *he,* she'd come up with the wrong one.

"An example that's interesting for people who're writing parsing programs," Riesbeck said, "is the show where she's at home and there's all these flowers around the room, and Blanche comes in—the next-door neighbor—and says, 'Gracie, where'd you get all these lovely flowers?' And Gracie says, 'Well, Helen was in the hospital, and George said I should visit her and take her flowers —so when she wasn't looking, I did!'

"Now, that's the kind of mistake a program ought to make," Reisback continued. "But why is it that it's a joke? Clearly you don't think of that as the average interpretation. When you go to a hospital, you have a script that says 'bring flowers.' Since you know you're supposed to bring flowers, you parse 'take her flowers' directly as 'take flowers to her.' That's an AI way of looking at it.

"But the hacker rewrites code a lot, and Bob rewrote code. You spend time trying to make the input/output very clean. You change a program so it'll look neater, not because it's absolutely necessary to get the job done. But the true hackers, like at Stanford and at MIT, were the people who'd been there for years. And one thing we didn't allow at Yale was hackers who'd be there for years, generating all sorts of nice software but never getting their theses done.

"To that extent, none of the students we've ever had were hackers, because it's always been their primary goal to get done. Certainly Bob was motivated enough that he wanted to finish up, because he really wanted to be a *person.* He wanted not to be a student, he wanted to be a faculty member somewhere. He had strong goals."

At Yale, science and engineering remained poor seconds to the humanities. The disdain was reflected in the history of the old Sheffield Scientific School, which was set up in the nineteenth century to offer professional training without the civilizing influence of Latin or Greek. The attitude was different at Berkeley.

During the Thirties and Forties, Berkeley was the birthplace of "big science," that awe-inspiring combine of big government and big war that developed at Ernest O. Lawrence's Radiation Lab. Lawrence, too, had come from Yale, a young physics professor whose scientific acumen was happily matched by his entrepreneurial skills. After building the first cyclotron, an eleven-inch accelerator that enabled physicists to study the particles inside the atom, he set up his Rad Lab in an unused shed in the shadow of the Campanile. A dozen years later, his 184-inch cyclotron in the hills was used to isolate U-235, the explosive uranium isotope that leveled Hiroshima.

Big science won the war, and big science set the precedent. If you wanted to be a scientist, you had to be an entrepreneur. Venture capital would be provided by the Pentagon. If you were lucky, a couple of foundations might come in as minor partners. But in the past few years all that has changed. It used to be that scientists were only expected to be entrepreneurs within the academic environment; now they're becoming entrepreneurs in the real world as well. This has caused heated debate and even led to disciplinary action against a handful of professors. Others have become millionaires as their high-tech start-ups have gone public with concepts developed in the lab. More typical is Schank's experience with Cognitive Systems, the company he set up in a downtown New Haven highrise: It hasn't made him a millionaire, but it hasn't endeared him to the Yale administration either.

I found Wilensky at his desk, working on his book. A dieffenbachia was growing on the table behind him, by the window overlooking the hills. No forks were buried with it, but its pot was in the shape of a computer terminal. I asked him how long it would be before he went into business.

He grinned. "Well, they say that tenure is a license to start a business these days. I don't know. I have ambivalent feelings about it, actually.

"There are a couple of reasons why I wouldn't do it. One of them is that I really do see all this, uh, avarice on the part of people like myself as being very destructive to scientific enterprise. Basically, I don't think the field is going to survive it—AI and cognitive science generally.

"I was watching the Oppenheimer thing last night—a televised biography of Robert Oppenheimer, the Berkeley physicist who led the A-bomb team at Los Alamos—"and at one point they mentioned that he didn't know the stock market had crashed until six months later. It struck me that this was the traditional paradigm of the scientist, this guy who's sort of lost from the world. What's funny is that it's so difficult today to find people who have this attitude. I think the whole environment where that attitude is possible is a thing of the past. It used to be the case that being a scientist had a certain degree more respect associated with it. Today it's lost some of that luster, and so people say, 'Why am I killing myself to become immortal? I'd rather be rich.' "

Wilensky shifted in his chair. "I love this business, you know? I like doing it. But every once in a while I turn around and I say, 'Ugh. Why should I be worried about getting eighty thousand dollars a year from NSF?' When you let your ego get unbounded, as it becomes in this game—if it wasn't already there to begin with —you say, 'Why should *I* have to worry about any of this? Why should *I* have to hustle two and a half million dollars from Sloan, when if I worked this hard for myself I could *become* the Sloan Foundation?'

"And the other thing that hits you is you think, Oh, this guy's consulting and he's earning this much money and I'm so much smarter than him and how could I let him do that? So you kind of feel you're stupid unless you're doing it. That's a pressure I admit to feeling, okay? But I haven't done anything about it yet for a number of reasons, not the least of which is that I can't afford to. Even if I were just completely rational, which I probably am not, the logical battle plan for me would be to get tenure at Berkeley and then go ahead and start the company."

I asked how he felt about hustling money from the military.

"Actually," he said, "ARPA and ONR [Office of Naval Research]—and ONR in particular—have been among the more enlightened funding agencies in the entire federal bureaucracy. They are large enough and broad enough that they can justify doing basic research on the grounds that results that will help anybody and everybody will help them, too. They don't really expect to see people build something that they will use. I have never done a single thing, nor do I intend to at this point, that has a military application per se. So in terms of day-to-day working environment, it really doesn't affect us. I don't say, 'Gee, I wonder what the military use of this is going to be.' I don't think about it."

What about the larger economic implications of AI—the impact it will have on the public at large?

He leaned forward and assumed a professorial tone. "Suppose AI worked—which it doesn't really. It does little things, but suppose we really built a natural-language interface so you can talk to your travel agent in natural language. There's a job that doesn't really require a very highly skilled person. In fact it's half-automated already—basically what you have is someone you talk to on the phone.

"My suspicion is that the vast majority of clerical jobs actually fall into that category—the travel agent, the airlines reservation clerk, certain other kinds of clerical personnel. Imagine if you took that kind of person and automated that. That's a very substantial part of the job market, particularly since the job market is becoming more service-oriented anyway. I don't think it's completely unfeasible that we could do those things within twenty years—and I think there's going to be a gigantic perturbation if it happens.

"The machines will be producing wealth, and the question is, Who's going to be using it? In some sense, the whole capitalist system is predicated on the notion that there are more and more people who want consumer goods. So in order for any of this to pay off, the barons of our industry are going to have some way of getting the wealth to the people so they can go ahead and buy all these useless goods.

"But if the means of production can be managed by a very small number of individuals, what do you do with all these people? Some people claim that our current modes of thinking will have to be rethought. We can't talk about capitalism versus socialism

143

anymore when no one has to work. I think there's a certain truth to that. I don't think we can end up with what we have now, where the needs of millions and millions of people are just not considered."

That leads to another problem, I remarked: the human fear of being replaced.

Wilensky was not sympathetic. "As far as AI is concerned," he said, "it's just a small symptom of a much larger problem. All the problems of alienation are general to our society. At this point, they're independent of what the new technology is. It's not clear to me that man was really well engineered for the society that he's developed." A smile crossed his lips as he thought of the *shtetl*. "My own feeling is that people were really meant to live in a village where you know everybody."

10

Sunday in Antioch

It was early April now, spring break. Faletti was alone in the office, updating his electronic address book. Kim had been down all morning. It had come up for a few minutes, but not for long. The systems people were putting in a new kernel today, the part of the operating system that works most directly with the machine's hardware. The office was dark. The lights were off, and it was gray outside.

The frame-based memory system Joe and Peter had been working on all through March had been completed a couple of days ago. It had been a simple matter, once that was done, to incorporate it into PANDORA's knowledge base—to fix it so that PANDORA's knowledge was stored in frames instead of in a series of if/then rules. Joe's plan for today had been to get started on a new project known as UC—the UNIX Consultant. Unfortunately, the installation of the new kernel was making it impossible for him to get much done. But he was using the time to think about UC, and about PANDORA's role in it.

UC was a product of Wilensky's desire to produce a big, useful AI system, a system with many different components all interacting to perform some real-world task. In this case, the task was to answer questions about UNIX. UC would serve as an intelligent assistant for people who were unfamiliar with the intricacies of the UNIX operating system. Instead of depending on other humans for help—humans who might not be handy, or who might be too busy, or who might think they were stupid for asking—these naïve users could query the computer directly.

Like all operating systems, UNIX is controlled by a series of coded commands. If you used the system every day, you'd know them by heart—but if you didn't, you'd be in trouble. Suppose, for example, you wanted to get rid of a file—an electronic document—called "filename." To do that, you simply type the command "rm filename." But if you didn't know that, you'd have a problem. You could look in the manual, but it could take half an hour to find the command. You could ask somebody who knows the system, but there might not be anybody to ask. With UC, however, you could simply ask the computer, in English. You could type in "How can I delete a file?" or "How do you remove a file?" or something like that, and it would tell you—also in English.

The way Wilensky was planning it, UC would consist of four main components. PHRAN and PHRED would translate from English to the computer's internal meaning representation and back again. The Context Model that Yigal was working on would keep track of any extended dialogue. And while simple requests like "How do you remove a file?" would get a canned response, more complicated queries would be sent to PANDORA for processing. PANDORA, the planning mechanism, would be equipped to deal with any eventuality.

To get him started, Wilensky had given Joe a specific question to work on: "I'm out of disk space, what do I do?" It was a situation familiar to any computer user. You're typing away, oblivious to the world around you, and the work you're producing bears the mark of sheer genius—which is fortunate, because it's five in the morning and you have to turn it in at nine. At last you're done. But as soon as you give the command to store it all on disk—on the magnetized plate that's whizzing around inside the computer—the "disk full" message flashes on the screen. Immediately you invoke the Panic frame. How do you save your work? What do you do? You ask UC.

This is a question that's complicated enough to bring in PAN-DORA. The way Wilensky saw it, PANDORA would consider the problem and come up with a solution, which it would then pass on to PHRED for communication to the user. But Joe wasn't entirely happy with this approach. He didn't like the idea that as a component of UC, PANDORA would simply be handed its goals —in this case, the goal of figuring out how to store a file on a full disk. After all, the real heart of PANDORA—the part he was proudest of, and the part that was most original in terms of AI research—was its goal-detection mechanism. It was one thing for a computer program to understand the goals of humans, as PAM had done; it was quite another for a program to come up with goals of its own.

So Joe decided it would be easier at this stage if he thought of the user as PANDORA itself. That way the goal of saving the file would be its own. Later on he could turn PANDORA into a UC component and program it with the knowledge that when asked a question, it should have the goal of answering it. That way its goal-detection mechanism would come into play. "I want to give PANDORA a situation where it's carrying out a goal," he explained. "A problem arises, and I want PANDORA to deal with it—but as a goal conflict, not as a question."

He went back to work, which meant staring out the window and occasionally scribbling things down in a spiral notebook. A half-hour or so later, Wilensky popped in from his office around the corner. He wanted to know how Joe was doing.

"Well, I've come up with a solution to the problem," Joe replied, standing up from his desk and digging his hands into his pockets. "First you find out if you have any files you want to delete. If you don't, then as a temporary solution you store it in a temporary file space. Then you mail it to yourself."

Wilensky nodded approvingly. Then Joe mentioned his problem with the disk-space example. "I don't think this is the way to do it," he said. "You've got to have it so PANDORA has a goal conflict. If you just have a simple question with no goal conflict, it could say, 'Quit and go home!'"

Wilensky didn't care how Joe handled it. He just wanted it done. There was the AAAI Conference in Pittsburgh this summer (AAAI is the American Association for Artificial Intelligence), and the deadline for submitting papers was April 15. Joe was planning to write a paper on PANDORA, and Wilensky wanted to do his on UC. "If you can get it to the point where it could do this example in a couple of days, that would be good," he said. "I want to have this for the paper."

That weekend, however, Joe was going home to Antioch for a Sunday afternoon volleyball game and an evening with his family. UC would have to wait.

It was eleven o'clock on a Sunday morning when I pulled up at Joe's. He lived in a typical Berkeley apartment complex, a block-long, low-rise structure with a basement garage and outdoor stairways leading motel-style to the apartments. The University Avenue commercial strip was a block away, and on the side streets were modest bungalows of the type this building had replaced. Basically a warehouse for humans, I thought as I climbed the concrete stairs and walked down the tired-looking corridor to Joe's door. Inside, however, the apartment was pleasant and cozy.

"It's a little bit plastic, actually," Joe said apologetically, "but that's because the landlord owns six buildings in Berkeley, each of which has the same green carpet and the same white walls." In fact I'd barely noticed the carpet beneath all the furniture. An old sofa, a Danish-modern chair, some end tables, a desk, and a battered piano were all crowded into a modest living room that gave onto a tiny balcony through a sliding glass door. Next to the desk was a wine rack that supported an Oxford English dictionary and a statuette of Snoopy. Three M. C. Escher prints were taped to the wall above the sofa; on the opposite wall, next to the piano, was a poster-shop Picasso of Don Quixote on horseback, carrying a lance.

Joe laughed when I asked him about it. "I've had that since my freshman year at Berkeley," he said. "My first quarter as a grad student, I went into my adviser's office and he had a copy of it. I said I really liked that poster and he asked me why. I didn't really have an answer, and he said, 'Well, is it maybe because you like fighting windmills?' And I said, 'Well, maybe!'"

The Falettis, I discovered as we left Berkeley, were a working-class family who'd come to America from northern Italy around the turn of the century. Most of the time since they'd spent in coal mines and steel mills. Joe's father has worked in accounting at the Pittsburg works of U.S. Steel since the day he got out of high school. He started out as a clerk; during the Fifties, he learned how to program computers in machine language. In those days, steel was manufactured at Pittsburg in open-hearth furnaces—huge brick-lined caldrons where scrap metals and iron were boiled for hours with aluminum, molybdenum, and other metals at temperatures approaching 3,000 degrees. Steel cable from the Pittsburg works was used to suspend the Golden Gate Bridge; flat-roll steel was used to make stoves, refrigerators, hot-water heaters, siding. But open-hearth furnaces became obsolete as new steel-making technology was developed, and then environmental-protection laws started forcing them to shut down. The floor where they stood was turned into a storage area; all they do in Pittsburg now is finishing work on the seven-and-a-half-ton steel coils that come in by rail from the Geneva works in Provo, Utah.

Besides his father and his grandfathers, Joe had two uncles who worked in the mill, and two of his five brothers worked there during the summers to put themselves through college. Joe himself preferred part-time jobs. He worked in the library when he was in high school, and for a while he thought about becoming a librarian. "Actually," he said, "ever since I was a little kid, when I was asked what I wanted to be when I grew up, I always said 'a lifetime student'—and I've certainly succeeded at that so far."

We were coming out of the Caldecott Tunnel by this time, a deep bore through the Berkeley Hills. The air on the other side was hotter and drier than anything along the bay. It would be hotter and drier still before we arrived. Antioch is only forty miles northeast of Berkeley, but that's two ridges and three climates away.

At thirty, Joe was the oldest of the family. The next-oldest, Steve, had a master's in math from San Jose State and was teaching at a junior college in Silicon Valley. Tom, twenty-four, had studied mathematical sciences at Stanford before getting married and returning to Antioch to serve as youth minister at Holy Rosary, the Falettis' parish church. Andy and Paul were both undergraduates at U.C. Davis, and Dan was still in high school. Paul, like Tom and their mother, was a charismatic Catholic.

I asked Joe what his family thought about AI.

"My parents have always been supportive of whatever I wanted to do," he said. "When I said I wanted to be a lifetime student, they said 'Fine. If you can put yourself through school, you can do anything you want.' "

I mentioned that it seemed difficult to conceive of a religious perspective on AI. The expression on his face told me he'd had this discussion before.

"There are those who say there's a soul, and therefore AI is impossible," he said. "And you can't argue with that position. All you can do is build a program. But even if I'm wrong, I'm going to have a hell of a lot more fun finding out I'm wrong than if I just said, 'Oh, well, I'll do something else.' "

"Is that why you do it—because it's fun?"

"Um-hum. There's absolutely no doubt that it's fun."

"What makes it fun?"

"Well, solving problems is always fun, and AI is a really hard problem, and—I dunno. Why is it fun? Why is anything fun? In the long run, a lot of your goals arise from whatever it is that gives you pleasure, and it's hard to say why any intellectual pursuit gives you pleasure. And yet I need to represent that in a program. Even my simple raincoat example—why does PANDORA wake up in the morning wanting to know what's going on in the world? What difference does it make to know that there's going to be an election in El Salvador and a rightist might actually win?

"But I'd rather work hard at something that's impossible than assume it's impossible and not do it. I generally find that people say something's impossible because they don't know how to do it. And the guys who do the impossible are the ones who believe there must be a way and work on it."

I asked if he had any religious impulses himself.

"Well, I was raised as a Catholic," he said, "but I have an awful lot of doubts at this point. I guess my main problem with religion is that a lot of people use it to do bad things instead of good things. But most of my family is quite religious, so I prefer not to let it be an issue. We don't talk that much about it. My uncle recently told me about Hal Lindsay's theory that Revelations is coming true in the next eighteen months and the world's going to end. And my reaction to that was, 'He can't do that! I haven't finished inventing a human yet.' "

We'd crossed the second set of hills and were speeding across a broad, sloping plain. On our left was the river, brown like the earth but roiling with whitecaps. On our right were the mountains, golden yellow in the harsh noonday sun. A hot, dry wind was whistling through the car. Power lines punctuated the landscape. A cluster of condos materialized on the horizon, loomed straight ahead, took shape around us.

"This is Antioch!" Joe sat up in his seat and looked around in wonder. "When I was in high school, everything around us was empty field."

Humans, I thought. They can get nostalgic about anything.

"You're gonna wanna take A Street. It's right after the G Street exit." G Street was coming up. "The center part of Antioch is really reasonably designed. There's A Street going out to L and First Street at the river coming up to Twentieth. But then they didn't continue it."

A few more turns brought us to the street where Joe had grown up. What once had been an almond orchard had some two decades before been transformed into a residential thoroughfare lined with modest ranch-style homes. The Falettis' was a tan stucco house with dark brown trim. A camphor tree was growing in the front yard. In front of the garage was Myrtle, a bright yellow nine-passenger 1961 Chevrolet Brookwood station wagon. Once the family car, Myrtle had devolved to Joe. Right now, however, she was grounded with a transmission problem.

Joe's dad emerged from the garage, a sturdy, gray-haired man with a broad smile and an easy manner. He was engaged in his favorite Sunday afternoon activity: tinkering. He had the back off an old black-and-white TV and was trying to fix it. Joe joined in immediately.

The TV was on a pool table, in a little cleared space surrounded by a heap of lampshades, electrical equipment, jigsaw puzzles, and cake mixes. The wall beside it was lined with books, board games, and canned food. There was an old upright piano against the other wall, and next to that a refrigerator and a freezer. The rest of the garage was stacked high with books and records and trunks and boxes.

As soon as they finished with the TV, Joe and his dad turned their attention to a beaten-up little record player on a table next to the piano. Somebody had donated it for the parish teen-agers to use in the church basement, but it hadn't worked in years. Joe's dad unscrewed the housing assembly and pulled out the turntable mechanism. The two of them worked on it intently for half an hour, turning it this way and that, studying its gears, arguing about its workings. It was a puzzle, and they puzzled it out. Then they put the whole thing back together and set about rounding people up for the volleyball game. Joe's mom and his brother Paul had gone to Oakland for a charismatic mass, but everybody else was ready to play.

The game was played in back of the church, on an asphalt court next to the school where Joe had learned to read and write. Holy Rosary is a modern-looking structure built of beige stucco and golden granite, with stained-glass windows and a free-form tower that looks like a flying nun's hat, or maybe a giant air scoop. "I don't know what you call it," Joe said when I asked him about the tower, "but it's ninety-two feet tall."

Steve and Dan are the athletic members of the family—Dan, in fact, was filling up the living room with his high-school basketball trophies—but volleyball was something all of them could enjoy. Even Joe, who used to read books during recess as a grade-school student, showed good reflexes on the court. Not that it mattered; the game was played more for fun than for points.

But some time later, while Steve and Dan were throwing a softball back and forth in the backyard and their dad was tinkering with something else in the garage, a small controversy erupted in the kitchen. Joe's mom was slicing kohlrabi for dinner (dinner was homemade pizza and a salad), when she suddenly realized that she wasn't sure if kohlrabi was a root or a tuber. She thought one thing, and Joe thought something else, but neither one of them was sure, and finally Joe ran to the living room to find out. He came back with a dictionary, but the definition wasn't precise enough.

Tom was in the living room. "What are oats made of?" he called out facetiously. By then the pizza was ready.

There were several pizzas, each one on a large cookie sheet. One by one Mrs. Faletti pulled them out of the oven and laid them on the kitchen table. Then she brought out her electric knife and handed it to Joe. He flicked it on and applied it to the first pizza. There was a grinding metallic noise as the blade hit the pan. He winced and pressed on. The pizza parted. Then he got to the edge. He tried it first from one angle, then from another. There seemed to be no way of slicing through the crust without slicing through the side of the pan as well.

"Maybe you should try something else," his mom said a little anxiously.

"This'll do," Joe declared, gritting his teeth. He lifted the hot pizza with his fingers and held it away from the pan. That did it. He waved his fingers in the air and started on the next slice. Five minutes later he was finished.

After dinner, while Sonia and Dan watched the Indianapolis 500 on TV in Joe's old room, the talk in the living room turned to the Postal Service. Mrs. Faletti wanted to know how the machinery in the post office reads addresses. "Do they just read zip codes?" she asked.

"They just read zip codes," Joe said.

"Well, how about when you have a seven that looks like a four?"

"They make a mistake."

"But how do they know where to look?"

"Well, first of all, you're supposed to put the the zip code far enough away from the address that it sort of stands out. And the only thing they know how to recognize is numbers, so everything else is garbage."

This led to a discussion of how the envelopes are fed into the zip-code-reading machinery, which led to an assessment of how much mail is junk mail, which led to a comparison of the U.S. Postal Service with the postal services of other countries, which led to a series of anecdotes about letters that were mailed and never received. After that, Mrs. Faletti wanted to know how left-handed people are supposed to open mayonnaise jars. She opens them left-handed herself, and she'd been having trouble with it.

Paul, Tom, Steve, Joe, and their dad all gathered around the kitchen table with a bunch of empty jars to figure out the mechanics of the matter. They unscrewed the tops again and again, monitoring their wrists and thumbs to see how it worked. They were laughing, but they were serious as well.

"How'd you say you normally do it?" Tom looked intently at his mom. "Use your left hand on the lid?"

"That's the only way," she declared.

"He's turning the jar," Tom cried, pointing to Joe.

"That wouldn't work! That wouldn't work!"

"I'm watching this hand," said Mr. Faletti, who was standing on Joe's right. "It's moving, too."

"It's moving," Joe admitted, "but the main movement is *here*, in the left hand. This is the grasping for me, and this is the turning."

"I think your thumb is where you really have your pressure," Mr. Faletti declared.

Tom decided to try it. "So I'm using my thumb to push on the jar—"

"Push . . . push . . . good!"

"Okay, it's got nothing to do with the strength in the arm," Tom said. "Dad figured it out. It's got to do with your thumb. That thumb controls all the action. That thumb gives you all the power."

"Look at the way I open the jar," Mrs. Faletti said. "Is that wrong?"

"That's wrong."

"That's why I can never open the jars!" She tried to do it their way.

"That's right—turn around!"

"Now push away with your thumb!"

"I don't even know which way to turn!" She held it tight against her stomach and bent over almost double.

"There you go!"

"That's what the stomach is for," Joe said between sobs of laughter.

"She's got the stomach for it!"

After a while the cheers died down, and slowly the brothers went their separate ways. The last ones left were Joe and Tom, the engineer and the believer. They were dressed almost identically in bright yellow shirts and dark brown pants—the same color scheme, as it happened, that prevailed in the living room of the Faletti home. It was sometime after ten when they gathered in the corner for a duet. Tom played "Lord of Glory" on the piano, and Joe sang gently over his shoulder, and their mother looked on with contentment in her eyes.

Joe was back in the office the next day, working on UC. That morning he'd come up with a way of formulating the disk-space example that mirrored the newspaper-in-the-rain problem. Instead of telling PANDORA it was morning, he said it was afternoon, and then he gave her a rule that said if it was afternoon, it was time to start writing a paper. When she finished the paper, PANDORA would discover she was out of disk space. Then she would have a goal to detect and a problem to solve.

Wilensky dropped in about two in the afternoon to see how Joe was doing. He seemed charged with excitement. He paced the room like a man on edge. "I'm really excited about this UC stuff," he told Joe. "I wanna come in every day and say, 'What new sentences does it understand?' I wanna . . . "

Joe flashed me a grin after he left. "And what did baby say today?" he quipped. Then he chuckled and turned back to his terminal.

11

The Chinese Room

The Israeli invasion of Lebanon was still some months away, but the conflict in the Middle East was already beginning to spill over into Berkeley's AI effort. On the wall outside the office, Yigal had posted some clippings from *Ha'aretz* and the *Jerusalem Post*. The articles were critical of official violence in the occupied territories —of campaigns against the Druze in the Golan Heights, of the "Pogrom-like atmosphere" caused by soldiers bursting into Palestinian refugee camps on the West Bank. Marc, who supported the Israeli government, objected vehemently.

And so Yigal came into the office on Monday to find a note from Marc on his desk. "Yigal," the note read, "As I also have my name on the door of this office and would (a) rather not have this type of propaganda associated with my name and (b) would rather not see it myself, I would appreciate it if you not post this type of information on our office door."

Yigal was irritated. He felt—and Joe agreed with him—that the little room at the back of Evans was more than just an office. In some sense, at least, it was their home as well. And since it was their home, they ought to be able to put what they wanted on the walls.

But Marc didn't buy it, so Yigal proposed a compromise. The clippings would stay up, but next to them he would post a notice. The notice read:

NOTICE—The material below was put up by Yigal Arens, and he alone is responsible for it.

Viewed coldly, logically, both conflicts—the larger one in the Middle East, and the smaller one in Evans Hall—might have seemed incomprehensible except as the result of behavioral patterns etched deep in the reptilian brain. That is to say, both conflicts were biological in origin and innately human. There was, however, no nonhuman system then capable of manipulating the symbols of Arab-Israeli conflict—symbols like "violence" and "soldiers" and "Palestinian" and "refugee"—in such a way that the dispassionate light of reason could be brought to bear. PANDORA, for example, was still struggling with its raincoat.

"Suppose you have a belief that it's raining." John Searle stood at the head of the IHL Library and confronted his audience. A deeply tanned man with shaggy, steel-gray hair, he faced the room with a casual self-assurance that bordered on cockiness. He was remarkably rugged-looking for a philosopher, and he had a voice that filled the room. "Now, that belief is just something in your *head*. We don't even know where it is in your head. But let's suppose that the water is pouring down outside. What has this stuff in your head got to do with what's going on outside?"

It was a question philosophers have been asking for thousands of years. What is the connection between the world within and the world without—between reality and our perceptions of reality? Bishop Berkeley held that all our perceptions are placed in our heads by God and that the notion of "material substance" is therefore absurd. Samuel Johnson thought he could refute this argument by kicking a stone—but, as Berkeley would surely have pointed out, the pain in his foot could just as easily have been put there by God as by the substance of the stone. Is all of reality, then, just an illusion? No one really knows. All we can say for sure is that if it is an illusion, it's a remarkably consistent one.

"Now, let's suppose that you sure wish Sally would pour you another cup of coffee," Searle continued. "Again, that's just something in your head. Now, what's that got to do with Sally pouring you coffee? It ought to strike you as absolutely *amazing* that in order to talk about what's in your *head*, we have to talk about the state of the weather, what Sally's doing—why don't we just talk about what's in your head?

"Well, the obvious answer—and in philosophy it's important to ask dumb questions at the beginning, and these are *dumb questions* because in some sense we all know the answer. The problem is to get a sophisticated way of formulating answers to those dumb questions. And to start on that question is to say, 'Well, the reason that these things in your head can only be specified in terms of all that stuff that's going on out there with the weather and Sally and so on is that *that's what these things in the head do! That's what they're all about!* Their whole purpose is to represent *states of affairs in the world!*"

Searle stared defiantly at his audience. A nub of chalk rested in his right hand. The blackboard behind him was strewn with cryptic messages. He was in the middle of his cognitive-science lecture on intentional causation.

Causation—the philosophy of cause and effect—is Searle's special field. Why do we ask Sally for a cup of coffee? Why do we believe it's raining? Why does the sun come up in the morning? That's what's meant by causation. A branch of metaphysics, causation became a critical issue in the seventeenth century, when the Scientific Revolution—Newtonian physics, in particular—gave rise to a world view that depended on the regularity of the universe. No longer could earthly occurrences be explained as the mischievous doings of God or the devil. Things happen in our world in a regular and dependable fashion. Celestial bodies are drawn to each other by gravitational force. One billiard ball strikes another and the second one moves. Causation, Hume declared a few decades after Newton's death, is the "cement of the universe."

It was the Scotsman David Hume—philosopher, essayist, diplomat—who created the the dominant paradigm of causality. Hume believed that causation itself can be neither observed nor experienced—that the only thing we can observe is that one event always followed another. Searle thinks this is nonsense. His lecture was an attempt to show why.

To do that, he was focusing on intentional causation. Intentionality is a characteristic of mental states that are directed at the outside world. Hopes, fears, beliefs, desires—all these are intentional states, because all of them are directed at something. We hope that Sally will pour us more coffee, fear that she won't, believe that it's raining, desire that it stop. Other states of mind —pain, anxiety, depression—are not intentional, but vague and undirected. Intentional causation is the ability of a mental state to cause a result in the outside world.

Searle had arrived at the IHL Library that afternoon with a Styrofoam cup full of coffee. Seating himself at the table at the front of the room, he pulled a penknife out of his shirt pocket, stirred his coffee, closed the knife, and stuck it back in his pocket. So many people had come to hear him that they were spilling out of the room onto the rickety little stairway outside. He took a deep gulp of coffee and stared at the crowd.

"If somebody says to me, 'Why did you take that drink?' I might say I was thirsty," he declared. "And it isn't just that I was thirsty *and* I took a drink. No, I know for a fact that I took a drink *because* I was thirsty. That is, there seems to be some kind of causal relationship as part of the empirical fact of my experience. How can that be the case? I haven't observed a whole lot of regularities that enabled me to state that I took that drink because I was thirsty, and in fact I really don't give a damn about the regularities. I know perfectly well why I took the drink. I was thirsty!"

Searle finished his coffee and moved on to his arm. The action of raising your arm, he explained, actually has two components. There's the physical act of your arm going up in the air—the "bodily movement"—and the mental act of your trying to put it there—the "intention-in-action." Can you have one without the other? "In fact," Searle declared, "we have experiments which have done just that.

"A lot of people—but the most famous is Penfield—have stimulated the motor cortex with a microelectrode, and what they produce is body movements without any intentions-in-action. You know Penfield, he's the brain-stabber in Montreal." (He was referring to Wilder Penfield, the eminent Canadian brain surgeon and pioneer neuroscientist.) "In the textbook there are these *terrible* photographs where they've shaved the guy's head and cut a window in his skull, and then Penfield goes in there with a microelectrode. And Penfield says—I can pretty much quote him verbatim—'When I have caused the patient's arm to move,

I have invariably asked him about it.' Well, you'd think he'd *better* ask him about it, he's messing around inside the guy's *brain!* And Penfield then reports, 'Invariably the patient says, "I didn't do that, *you* did it!" ' "

Searle had to wait for the laughter to subside before continuing. "Now that's a case where we have a bodily movement without an intention-in-action. And there's a famous William James experiment where you have the intention-in-action without the bodily movement. In that case, they had a guy in a dark room and they anesthetized his arm. They ordered him to raise his arm and he did what he thought was carrying out the order, but they held his arm at his side and the guy was then amazed to discover that his arm didn't go up. He had something analogous to a hallucination —that is to say, he had an intention-in-action without a bodily movement.

"Now all of that is part of our experience," Searle concluded. "If you think about it, you don't just observe your arm going up, you experience your own raising it. It isn't just an observation you make that there's a causal nexus there. I want to say the causation is part of the actual content of the experience."

Searle beamed triumphant. His arm was white with chalk dust, the blackboard behind him strewn with half-erased diagrams. Immediately, as if to prove his point, a half-dozen arms went up in the air. People experienced an intention-in-action, and then they experienced a bodily movement. Searle gestured toward the first arm.

As always in these seminars, there was someone in the room who didn't buy the argument. This one was a young man who didn't think Searle had actually said anything. What if Penfield told you to raise your arm at the exact moment that he stimulated your brain? What would you have then?

Searle was accommodating. "The point you're making I take to be the following," he said. "A guy might have all this stuff exactly the way I described it, and all the same it might not be functioning causally. And indeed, that seems to me exactly right. I might have exactly this experience—my arm go up—and unknown to me, I didn't raise my arm. Wilensky's got an apparatus"—he gestured toward Wilensky, who was sitting innocently enough at the front of the room—"and as soon as the green light goes on that says I'm trying to raise my arm, he pushed a button and a magnet in the ceiling raises my arm because they've injected a whole lot of metal in my arm. I mean, that's a conceivable situation. And in a case like that, I would be having something analogous to an hallucination."

Wilensky sat up with a "who, me?" look on his face. Searle, smiling, gestured toward the next arm.

About the time Searle was speculating about Wilensky's designs on his arm, an essay he'd written on intentional states in computers appeared in a book called *The Mind's I.* The book was billed as a collection of ruminations on self and soul, and it had been put together by Daniel Dennett, a well-known philosopher at Tufts, and Douglas Hofstadter, the author of *Gödel, Escher, Bach.* Searle's essay, "Minds, Brains, and Programs," went to the heart of the debate over computerized thought. Does a computer program exhibit intentional states? Does it hope, fear, believe, desire? Could a computer have a mind? Those were the questions.

Searle began by describing a program of Schank's, the one that "understands" restaurant stories and then answers questions about them. (Understanding is an intentional state.) He proposed a *Gedankenexperiment,* a make-believe test. Suppose Searle himself were stuck in a room the way the computer is. Suppose he were given pieces of paper with Chinese symbols written on them, together with detailed instructions for manipulating these symbols. Suppose he got so good at following these instructions that, locked away in his room, he couldn't be distinguished from a native speaker of Chinese. And now suppose that, unbeknown to him, the people outside started feeding him strings of symbols they called "stories" and "questions" and eliciting responses they called "answers." What would we say then? Would we say Searle "understands" Chinese?

Of course not, Searle declared. Why, then, would we say a computer understands Chinese, or English, or anything else? Clearly what AI has produced is not computer understanding; at best it's a computerized simulation of understanding. "No one supposes that computer simulations of a five-alarm fire will burn the neighborhood down or that a computer simulation of a rainstorm will leave us all drenched," he wrote. "Why on earth would anyone suppose that a computer simulation of understanding actually understood anything?"

This was Searle's infamous "Chinese room" argument. When first published, in a scholarly journal called *Behavioral and Brain Sciences,* it had set off an intellectual firestorm in the AI community. No less than twenty-seven responses had been printed with it. In the "Reflections" that followed it in his book, Hofstadter tried to rebut it single-handedly.

In the first place, Hofstadter argued, it was misleading to suggest that a human could manipulate symbols in this way. But even if you bought that argument, you'd have to say it wasn't the man in the room who understood Chinese but the whole system— man, instructions, and everything. It didn't matter that the man in the room was a conscious being; he would be just a small part of the thing that really did the understanding. "Minds exist in brains and may come to exist in programmed machines," Hofstadter concluded. "If and when such machines come about, their causal powers will derive not from the substances they are made of, but from their design and the programs that are run in them. And the way we will know they have those causal powers is by talking to them and listening carefully to what they have to say."

Hofstadter's response was the "systems reply" that Searle had already attempted to refute in his essay. Searle's response to that was to review the entire volume in the *New York Review of Books.* He ignored most of the book, but he did lavish quite a bit of attention on Hofstadter's "Reflections" about his essay. Among other things, he charged Hofstadter and Dennett with deliberately fabricating a quotation and then using that quotation as the basis of their argument against him. They said he'd described the symbols and instructions given to the man in the room as "a few slips of paper"; actually, he'd referred to them as "bits of paper."

But the main thrust of Searle's review, which was titled "The Myth of the Computer," was his dismissal of "the nonsense talked about computers nowadays." The computer, he argued, is just a tool, not a brain nor a threat to those who have them. It can't have mental states because it doesn't have the causal powers (that is, the neurons and the neurotransmitters) that the brain has. Imagine a computer made out of old beer cans instead of electronic circuits. In principle, it would be possible to build such a device;

in practice, the results would be rather clunky. But if a computer made of old beer cans told you it was thirsty, would you believe it?

Predictably, Searle's review prompted an angry reply from Dennett, categorically denying any intentional falsification and declaring that the argument still held, misquote or no misquote. Searle then dashed back to his typewriter to draft a reply to the reply . . . and so it went, squabble and metasquabble and meta-metasquabble, an endless spiral of academic rancor.

Does a computer have mental states? Can it understand Chinese? "Well, the easiest way to tell if a system has mental states," Searle declared, "is to be that system." We were seated in his office in Moses Hall, a book-lined room looking out across a wooded hillside. The windows were dappled with sunlight. "That's how I know I've got mental states! Now, you can't do that with every system, so when I want to get at other people's mental states, I have to do it indirectly. But that doesn't mean it's mysterious or unverifiable.

"See, I put that beer-can fable in there because there you can think, or at least I think, that it would just be *crazy* to think a beer can has mental states, because it's the wrong kind of stuff. A lot of people who read that article thought, These guys can't really say what you say they say. They must be putting us on. They really think computers have thoughts and feelings? 'Yeah,' I said, 'they really think that.' "

"So what you're saying," I asked Searle, "is that only biological organisms can have mental states?"

"Or some reasonable facsimile. You know, I don't say we couldn't build a robot in the lab that had mental states—but what we'd have to do would be to duplicate the causal powers of the brain. Now, maybe we could do that in some other medium. You know, maybe Martians have mental states but they have green slime in their brain, and we say, 'What the hell! Why build these damn neurons? It's a lotta work! Let's build green slime!' And it might work.

"But there's really two principles. One is, the brain does it, so if anything else is gonna do it, it's gotta be as powerful as the brain. And secondly, no computer, just in virtue of instantiating a computer program, can do it. It's gotta have more than just a computer program. And I think it's very unlikely that we will be able to synthesize mental states without employing the kinds of mechanisms the brain uses.

"I would take the mind to be a biological phenomenon. Of course, there's no reason why you couldn't reproduce the biological basis of the mind, just as you can reproduce the biological base of any other biological phenomenon. After all, biology is a branch of chemistry! And chemistry is a branch of physics! So there must be some way to do it! But in order to do it, you've got to do what the brain does—and computers don't do that. All they do is a formal description of what the brain does. Hang on just a second."

Someone was knocking at the door. Searle opened it to find a scraggly-looking young man with the look of the devil in his eyes. He had long, frizzy hair and a ragged coat. He was hunched over to one side, and in his right hand he was clutching a tennis racket. "Oh, hi," Searle said warily. "I can't talk to you now. Okay? Go talk to the authorities." He chuckled softly at his joke.

His visitor was not to be put off so easily. "Can I get an appointment to see you next week?"

"I'm on sabbatical." That ought to work. "Next week I'm going to Chicago."

"Can I go with you?"

"*No!*"

"But I grew up in Chicago! I know that town better than anybody!"

"I don't wanna see the town!"

"Can I come back in twenty minutes?"

"Half an hour." Searle closed the door, shoulders drooping. "That guy drives me crazy," he muttered under his breath. "Absolutely crazy. Where the hell were we? Oh, yeah. What the computer does is a formal representation of real phenomena, and it's a mistake to think that a formal simulation is the real thing. Nobody makes that mistake where fires or thunderstorms are concerned. What do we do when we do photosynthesis in the laboratory? Well, what they do is they try to duplicate the actual biochemistry. They don't put it on a computer!" He gave a snort of incredulity. "It's just crazy to think that the computer has got thoughts and feelings and worries the way you and I do. It hasn't got a brain!"

Sort of like the scarecrow in *The Wizard of Oz*, I thought. But does that really make any difference? In terms of the effect it will have on human life, what will it matter if computers have mental states or not?

"What does it matter? It depends on what the question is. If we're talking about the impact of computers on our lives, that might be the same whether they have mental states or not. Certainly. But when we're talking about *psychology,* when we're talking about the computer as a device to study human beings, it matters enormously whether the computer uses the same principles that human beings use, or whether it just simulates the input and output of a human being. There are a lot of machines that do that. We have machines that dig ditches and wrap books and all kinds of things, but we don't think they have any psychological interest.

"Now, a lot of people have the impression that I'm opposed to the computer or that I'm sneering at programming. That's not true at all. I have enormous admiration for the amount of effort and intelligence that goes into this work. I just don't want its results to be misinterpreted. And there's a lot of nonsense that comes out about AI, like the idea that computers are a deep threat to human beings and that computer achievement will destroy our sense of human dignity. That's *crap!* I have a pocket calculator that can beat any mathematician in the world, but that's no threat to anybody's dignity. It's just a device we use as a tool. As I say in that article, I'm not threatened by ditchdiggers. A mechanical ditchdigger can outdig a whole army of people, but we don't feel our ditchdigging dignity has been threatened. It's just absolute nonsense!"

I got to the fifth floor of Evans just as the bedeviled tennis player was leaving Wilensky's office. I asked Wilensky who he was. "I don't know," Wilensky said. "I'm beyond caring anymore. I find that the most important thing is to discourage them from coming. So I told him my next appointment was in the fall, and he said, 'When?' I said I didn't know, and he said, 'How about September fifteenth?'"

I mentioned that Searle seemed to be saying that artificial intelligence is only a simulation.

"There's an appealing aspect to his position," Wilensky replied, "because it's very intuitive, okay? Unfortunately, I find that appealing to intuition really isn't enough here because, as science has pointed out time and time again, intuitions are often wrong.

"Let's take the initial argument he made, which is, Can something simulated be the real thing? Obviously if you're simulating it, it ain't the real thing. If you're simulating a rainstorm, to use a Searle example, you ain't gonna get drenched—so why is it that when you simulate understanding, you're gonna get real understanding?

"The answer to that is, It depends. It's not the case that all simulations are not the real thing. If you're interested in aerodynamics, you simulate winds by creating a wind tunnel. Those aren't real winds, but you get knocked over by them just as surely as you get knocked over by standing on the wing of a plane in flight.

"Now, it certainly is the case that if a computer program simulated photosynthesis, it wouldn't produce sugar. Why is it that if it simulates intelligence, it should literally produce understanding? If the essential quality of understanding was that it was done by a human acting in the normal way, then sure, the computer simulation isn't going to handle it—but that would be your assumption to begin with. On the other hand, if what we mean by *understanding* is some sort of logical construction that anything can do, then if you preserve that logical structure you might in fact be preserving the essential thing that is understanding. It's not at all clear, unless you presume to begin with what the essential nature of understanding is.

"Now, I would argue that our intuition about understanding is that it's much closer to being this funny logical thing than a biological process. The claim for that is really Searle's own argument. If I said to you, 'A computer that simulates photosynthesis doesn't produce sugar,' you laugh. It's not even close. But if I said to you, 'A computer that simulates understanding is really understanding something,' you don't think so but you're not really sure. Well, if understanding is so obviously a biological process, why isn't it *obvious* to you that the computer isn't understanding, the same way it's *obvious* to you that it's not producing sugar? Well, the answer is that it's obvious that photosynthesis is a physical process, but it's not so obvious that understanding isn't this logical process. So it seems to me that the simulation thing is actually a red herring.

"That's one problem. Then there's this whole other notion he mentioned—'Well, look, obviously a computer that's simulating pain doesn't feel pain.' Certainly that's a very intuitive position. But it's a very problematic position philosophically, in a way that Searle's philosophy doesn't even let him ask.

"Forget AI for the moment. Let's take something a little less problematic, like biology. Certainly you don't believe that neurons experience pain. Certainly you don't believe that the carbon, hydrogen, and oxygen that make them up experience pain. Yet science has told us the *incredible* and counterintuitive fact that if you take the ordinary molecules that are sitting around in this room and put them in the right configuration, they will feel pain.

"Now that's *crazy!* If anyone told you that, you'd have to laugh at them. But it's true. And there's a name for that in philosophy. It's the problem of emerging properties. How is it that something that you don't think of as having those properties can all of a sudden emerge with those properties? There's a mystery there, and it's a mystery that also applies to computers.

"There used to be a debate within science between vitalism and mechanism—an argument over whether there was living stuff and nonliving stuff, or whether it was the same stuff arranged two different ways. The vitalists, who believed that you were made out of different stuff than the bookcase, said, 'Look, it's kind of obvious, you know, that this unliving stuff doesn't ever become living, and there's all this intuitive evidence that what you are is completely different from this other stuff.' And the mechanists said, 'Oh, it's the same thing, it's just kind of arranged differently.' Clearly a stupid position.

"But in fact, the issue was resolved empirically with the synthesis of urea in the laboratory. Now we've actually made viruses in the laboratory out of chemicals on the shelf, and in fact the position which is accepted by most informed members of our society today is that we as people are made out of chemicals, and that there's nothing else in us that's special, and that if you took these chemicals and put them together you'd get a human being. The problem is knowing how to put them together.

"What I think is going on here is very much a vitalist/mechanist kind of argument. I think there's a real mystery here, and what I'd like to be able to do is ask the question. And the problem is that from Searle's point of view, you can't even ask the question."

Wilensky sat back and savored his position.

"I can tell you, by the way, what's wrong with the man-in-the-room argument. My response is what he called the 'systems position,' and his response to that is that you simply internalize the whole system. Well, it's wrong. You can use the same argument to prove that machines can't multiply numbers.

"Suppose I go over to John Searle and I say, 'Look, I want you to follow these instructions,' and they actually turn out to be the instructions for long division, which because of Searle's penchant for philosophy he's forgotten how to do. So he does the same kind of thing that he did before, but now he's actually doing long division. And then I go up to him and I say, 'John, do you know how to do long division?' and he says, 'I'm sorry, I've forgotten how.' So it's clear that the man doesn't know how to do long division. I would argue that since the man doesn't do long division, and there's no other candidate except the man acting in his normal way, long division didn't happen.

"Step back for a minute and see what's happening. The reason this is problematic is that it's very unusual in the ordinary world that you see a system within another system in this way. But in fact it does happen, and the computer happens to be an example of it. We implement a system that does text editing, but your computer's CPU doesn't come from the manufacturer *knowing* how to do text editing. If you actually looked at the computer running, it's still doing the same diddly-squat that it ever did. It's not doing text editing, it's doing add-this-number. And if you ask it, 'Did you do text editing?' it would say, 'No, I was just sitting here adding these numbers.'

"Now let's take a look at that from the point of view of the man in the room. Certainly the homunculus, the man in the room, doesn't have the experience of understanding—but it's not required for him to have it. The computer adding the numbers didn't *experience* text editing, it only 'experienced' the things it knows how to do—namely, adding the numbers. But if you look at the computer as a system with a program, that whole thing actually did real, bona-fide text editing.

"The problem here is that you don't think of the computer as having experiences. The man in the room does have experiences, so you tend to identify this system with the man in the room. But the fact that the man in the room has experiences is irrelevant to his role as a symbol manipulator. So in fact it's a trick. It's kind of like identifying the experiences of the person as the experiences of the neuron. It's as if each of your neurons could talk to you on the side, in addition to whatever else they did. When you say to them, 'Did you understand Chinese?' the neurons are gonna say, 'No, we're just sitting here bridging the synapses.' And you say, 'See, none of these guys inside your head understood Chinese, so you couldn't have understood Chinese.'

"There's a way I can get Searle to admit this, which is simply the following. I go over to him and ask him if he understands Chinese—*except* that instead of asking him in English, I write it on these funny little pieces of paper and shove it under the door! Okay? So if we really built a full system and I put these symbols under the door which happen to say in Chinese 'Do you understand Chinese?' I'll get back the answer '*Of course* I understand Chinese! What the hell do you think I've been *doing* for the last few hours? Are you *crazy?*' Okay? And then I ask John Searle in English, 'Do you understand Chinese?' and he says, 'I don't understand a word of it.' So there really are two systems there."

Wilensky gave a satisfied smile. "You know," he said, "at one point I said to John, 'I think the reason you believe all this, and the reason you believe certain scientific theories that are far more contradictory to our intuitions than anything AI has to say, is because physics works and AI doesn't—yet. But if you were surrounded by smart machines and you were talking to them all the time and they were answering you back, then we wouldn't be having this argument.' "

In the office around the corner, Joe was working on his UC examples for PANDORA. How do you delete a file? You ask the computer, and it answers you back: "Typing 'rm filename' will remove the file with name filename from your current directory." The man in the room understood nothing but machine language—binary digits, zeros and ones, yes and no—but the system was understanding English. Or at least processing English.

169

But deleting a file is a simple matter. What happens when you run out of disk space? At that point, UC ran into a slight snag. The problem was that PANDORA still didn't realize the person who'd run out of disk space was a human. PANDORA thought it had run out of disk space itself.

It no longer thought it had to write a paper because it was afternoon, however. Joe had decided that was too bizarre. Instead, he'd given it the goal of storing a new electronic mail address for PAMELA. This led PANDORA to figure out that it had to edit its electronic address book. But when it tried to do that, it got an error message saying it was out of disk space. It tried to delete some unneeded files, but there weren't any. So it stored the address book in temporary file space and mailed it to itself so it wouldn't get lost. Then it made a mental note to ask the system manager for more disk space.

A new electronic mail address for PAMELA? Wasn't that a bit incestuous?

"No!" Joe gave a sheepish laugh. "I think most people keep their sisters' addresses!"

12

On Deadline

The fifth-floor lounge was crowded with computer people. Once a month the computer science division invited a distinguished visitor to speak, and it was customary to begin these affairs with a little reception at which doughnuts and coffee were served. Today's visitor was Nils Nilsson, the director of AI research at SRI International.

SRI—the former Stanford Research Institute—is the leading nonacademic AI research site in the United States. Nilsson has been there since 1961. During the late Sixties he'd been in charge of its notorious Shakey project. Shakey was the world's first mobile robot, an ARPA-funded box on wheels that was designed to roll around the halls and stack blocks on top of one another. What made it notorious was an article in *Life* magazine, a sensationalistic report that billed it as "the first electronic person . . . a machine with a mind of its own." In fact, it was all Shakey could do to keep from running into walls. But that didn't deter the reporter, who imagined a computer take-over in the not-too-distant future and quoted MIT's Marvin Minsky as saying, "If we're lucky, they might decide to keep us as pets"—a remark Minsky has denied ever making.

Nilsson was on campus to talk about what SRI was doing now. He was also a little curious to find out what was happening at Berkeley, which was why he and Wilensky were in a corner discussing "Searleisms"—Wilensky's term for John Searle's belief system. Wilensky was trying to explain Searle's argument that computers lack the causal powers of the brain—the cells and chemicals that enable us to think and to understand. "Well," Nilsson retorted, "maybe silicon has other properties that allow machines to *grok* instead of to understand. What would he make of *that?*"

Wilensky didn't know. "His argument really rests on the following conclusions," he said. "It's certainly counterintuitive to think that computers would have those properties. It would be surprising if your computer got angry."

Nilsson screwed his face up as if he wasn't sure at all. *"IIII dunno!* I wouldn't be so surprised! It would surprise me if it happened *tomorrow,* but if it happened in twenty years, or fifty years, or a hundred years, it wouldn't surprise me. I don't think in principle it's impossible."

Wilensky was in complete agreement. "I think, though, I would have to summarize what John has to say by saying, 'Gee, it's sort of counterintuitive to think that things like this coffee machine here have the potential for experiencing fears, hopes, desires, and whatever. And since it's counterintuitive, it would be surprising if that turned out to be the case, and therefore—' "

"A lot of people have been wrong with those kinds of arguments in the past," Nilsson broke in. "It's rather surprising that the earth goes around the sun. It's counterintuitive, actually."

Wilensky agreed. Very counterintuitive indeed.

A few minutes later Zadeh ushered Nilsson to the basement of Evans, where a lecture hall had been reserved—a miniature amphitheater that was already nearly full. Dreyfus and Searle were in attendance, as were the members of the Berkeley AI group.

Nilsson strode down the aisle and took his place on the dais. He was a distinguished-looking man, tanned and poised, with watery blue eyes and silver hair and a silvery tweed jacket that accentuated his slender frame. He had the perfectly turned-out look of a corporate lawyer. No one would have taken him for a man who programs robots.

There were, Nilsson announced, several areas of AI research at SRI—vision, expert systems, natural language, and planning, in addition to robotics and other areas of computer science. The vision people were working with the robotics group to develop robot arc welders and circuit-board inspectors. They were also working with the expert-systems people to develop an artificial photo-interpreter for the Pentagon—a system that could compare digitized maps with digitized photographs to see if any new roads or airstrips had been put in. The expert-systems group had developed PROSPECTOR, the intelligent geologist that locates mineral deposits. The language group was working on a natural-language interface to enable business people to communicate with computers in English—a system not unlike Wilensky's UC project. And then there was a broader group that, like Joe and Peter, was working on knowledge representation and planning.

"We want to be able to develop a plan of action for accomplishing a certain goal," Nilsson said, pacing the stage with his hands in his pockets. "One thing we'd like to be able to do is state to the computer system a situation that we want to have brought about. For example, if you were thinking about a robotics system that might be able to clean the house, then you'd have to describe to that robot what it means for the house to be clean or the dishes to be washed or the floor to be swept or whatever. So we're interested in programs that can chain together sequences of actions that will take the world from the world we're in now to one which is described by this goal condition—from the world in which the room is messy to one in which the room is clean.

"Now, we have some support from the Air Force Office of Scientific Research and the Office of Naval Research, so we try to describe the work in terms that are relevant to our sponsors. There's a problem the navy has with planning the movement of airplanes on a carrier deck. They might have a mission in which several of these planes take off, and one of them might have to be brought up from the hangar deck but there's something else on the elevator, and some planes might be ready and others might not, and some of them might have to be fueled, so there are lots of details to be worked out. We've developed a program called SPOT that does that. "This program makes a plan and then supervises the execution of that plan. Of course, we don't *really* execute the plan at SRI because we don't have an aircraft carrier, but we can simulate it."

There was one last project Nilsson wanted to describe that day, one involving robots and common sense. If successful, it would give robots the first glimmerings of consciousness.

Humans experience consciousness as an everyday phenomenon, but few ever try to pin it down. Those who do—psychologists and philosophers, mainly—find it remarkably slippery. It seems to involve having a sense of yourself in relation to the world around you. It seems to depend on an understanding of the difference between the world within and the world without—between reality and your perceptions of reality. In *Gödel, Escher, Bach,* Douglas Hofstadter describes it as the "strange loop" of the self reflecting upon the self. If this is correct, then consciousness is really metamind—the mind looking down at the mind.

Nilsson didn't explain his project in terms so grand, but the crux of it was to give robots a sense of themselves, and a sense of other robots as well. "Here we're imagining that we've built all these robots," he said, "and we're focusing on one of them—let's say R1." He started drawing robots on the blackboard behind him.

"Now, we want to be able to represent in R1's computer certain information about the world. In particular, we want R1 to have some information about what R2 believes. Suppose it is the case

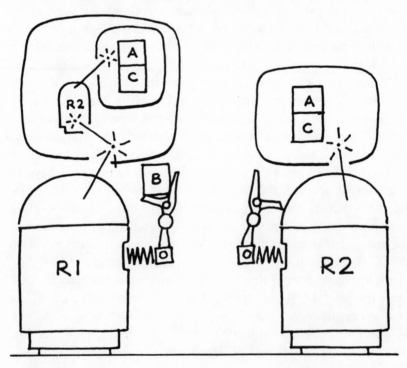

that R2 actually believes that block A is on block C. We might want R1 to believe that R2 believes that A is on C." As he spoke, the first of several robot diagrams took shape.

"One of the frontiers of artificial intelligence," Nilsson continued, "is looking at formulations which are actually inspired by work in philosophy of how to represent knowledge about other people's knowledge. In this case, other robots' knowledge. Now this gets rather complicated, as you might guess." He started drawing more robots on the blackboard.

"Now, R1 may know that block A is on block C—and, of course, we have to have a way of saying that R1 knows that it knows that block A is on block C—and it might believe that R2 believes that C is on A. And R1 is a very helpful robot, let's say, and it wants to stamp out error wherever it occurs, so it wants to change R2's beliefs. Following some of the work in speech acts that has been taken up by people in artificial intelligence, we might imagine that one of the ways R1 might affect R2's beliefs is by a speech act"—Nilsson permitted himself a slight smile here—"and that act would be to inform R2 that A is on C. And so R1 utters this

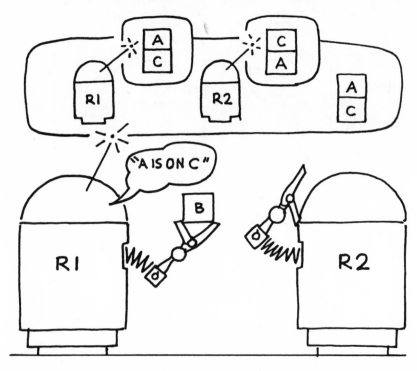

statement—not in English, but in some robotic precise talk which we'll invent."

By this time, Nilsson had completed a second diagram which showed the state of affairs in R1's mind. It showed R1's model of the world, it showed R1's model of its model of the world, and it showed R1's model of R2's model of the world as well.

"So R2, on hearing this, has several options. R2 can merely believe that R1 said this. Or R2 could trust R1 and begin to believe that A is on C. Or it could believe that R1 merely wants R2 to believe that A is on C. There are whole levels of indirectness that have to be analyzed. It might be that R2 is actually smarter than R1 thinks—that R2 really believes that A is on C and knows that A is on C, but thinks that R1 thinks that R2 thinks that C is on A and merely says, 'I know.'"

This final remark was greeted with uproarious laughter—just as Nilsson had expected it would be. He had a gleam in his eye as he put down his chalk and asked if there were any questions.

David Chin had one. "There are two different approaches to AI," he said. "One is where you look at how human beings work,

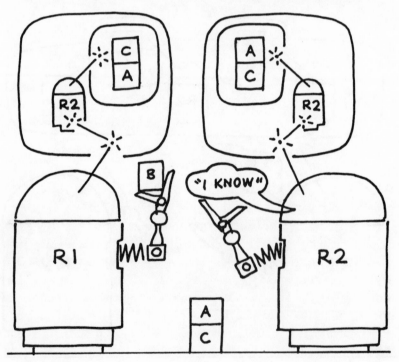

and the other is the engineering approach. What's yours?"

Nilsson grinned. "We'd like to do it any way we can," he said.

On the second day of spring quarter, some forty undergraduates were lined up outside the AI office, most of them sitting cross-legged on the floor. They were waiting to see a computer science professor whose office was in the corner. They were there to make their "41 appeals"—appeals to get into CS 41, a course in machine structures that's a prerequisite for the upper-division courses in computer architecture that all CS majors are required to take. But to take the machine-structures course, you had to get an account on one of the division's PDP-11 minicomputers, and only a few of these accounts were available. It was a familiar problem in computer science—too many students, too little room. It was so familiar, in fact, that the Engineering School had an assistant dean whose main job was to talk would-be computer science majors into trying some less crowded field, like civil engineering. He wasn't having much success; computer science was where the jobs were, which was why these people were sitting in the hall.

Joe picked his way through the throng and walked into the office. His plan for today was to get PANDORA to work. There was not much time. The AAAI deadline was little more than a week away, and he had to write his paper yet. But first, PANDORA, using the frame-based memory system he and Peter had recently completed, had to put on her raincoat and pick up the newspaper.

Peter and Yigal were already at work. Joe grunted in their direction and headed straight for his little desk by the window. Within seconds he'd logged into Kim and loaded the PANDORA program. He was a bit tense. This would be PANDORA's trial run.

He typed in the "nextevent" command and started PANDORA on its loop. The screen before him filled up with green lettering. He nodded approvingly as the lettering scrolled before him. Everything was going according to plan. The TimeOfDay was Time Morning and the Weather was Condition Raining. Without hesitation, PANDORA found its normal plan. It had to PTrans to Location Outside. It had to Grasp the Object Newspaper. It had to PTrans to Location Inside.

177

Next it went through the motions in simulation mode. As soon as it got to the first step, a new goal went into its goal stack. It was the ResolveGoalConflict metagoal: Having automatically detected the conflict between its original goal of PTransing to Location Outside and its built-in PreserveDryness goal, it now had the new goal of resolving the conflict between them. It waited for the next command. Joe typed in "go."

On cue, PANDORA found the normal plan for resolving its goal conflict. The normal plan was to PutOn its Object Raincoat. It simulated this to anticipate its effects and put it at the top of the plan stack. Now it was ready to execute its plans.

Up until this point, all PANDORA had done was to find the appropriate plans and run through them in its "mind." Then it put them in its FuturePlans stack. Now it was ready to go through that stack and carry them out—to put on its raincoat and pick up the paper. Of course, it wasn't really going to do anything of the sort. It was only a computer program—a sequence of commands in Franz Lisp, Opus 38, plus PEARL; a string of zeros and ones that had been arbitrarily divided into thirty-two-bit "words"; a series of positive and negative impulses that had been read off a whirring magnetic disk and were now zipping through the circuitry of a computer named Kim No-VAX in the chilly isolation of the fourth-floor machine room. But PANDORA didn't know that. It didn't know anything except what Joe had programmed it to know, and the only thing Joe had programmed it to know was what to do in the morning when it's raining.

Joe typed in the "go" command again. More writing scrolled across the screen:

```
New plan gotten from FuturePlans:
   (PutOn (Actor (Ego))
          (Effects ((Wearing (Object
                               (Raincoat))
                              (Person (Ego))))))
          (Object (Raincoat)))
Plan being executed:
   (PutOn (Actor (Ego))
          (Effects ((Wearing (Object
                               (Raincoat))
                              (Person (Ego))))))
          (Object Raincoat)))
```

```
New effect is:
  (Wearing (Object (Raincoat))
           (Person (Ego))))
```

PANDORA had put on its raincoat. So far, so good. Now it was ready to move on:

```
New plan gotten from FuturePlans:
  (PTrans (Actor (Ego))
          (Effects ((At (Object (Ego))
                        (Location (Inside))))))
          (Object (Ego))
          (To (Inside))
          (From (nilstruct)))
```

A stricken look passed across Joe's face. For some reason, PAN-DORA had PutOn its raincoat and then decided to PTrans *inside*. As Joe looked on, it continued to execute the remainder of its plan, Grasping the newspaper and then PTransing *outside*. He stared at the screen with the horrified expression of a man who has just watched his child spout gibberish and vomit green foam. After all this, PANDORA had gotten it backward. It had gone inside to pick up the newspaper, and then it had gone out in the rain to read it. Joe let out a low moan and turned toward the window.

It didn't take long to find the bug. The bug was in the plan stack. In computer programming, a stack is a sequence of instructions the program has to execute as it proceeds through its loop. It works just like a stack of trays in a cafeteria: Instructions are placed one-by-one on the stack, and the program starts with the one on top. (This is known as "pushing" and "popping.") Just as with the cafeteria trays, the last one down is the first one off. Because PANDORA had formulated the raincoat plan after the retrieve-newspaper plan, the plans in its plan stack had gone in as follows: PTrans outside, Grasp newspaper, PTrans inside, PutOn raincoat. When it came time to execute them, then, they came out in reverse.

Fixing the bug was not so simple. There is another way of organizing a program's instructions, and that's to put them in a queue. If a stack is like a stack of cafeteria trays, a queue is like a queue of people at a bus stop: The first in line is the first to get on, and the last in line is the last to get on. There was a problem with that, however: If PANDORA executed its plans in the same order it made them, it would end up putting on its raincoat after it came back inside with the newspaper. A plan queue, it seemed, wouldn't work any better than a plan stack.

What PANDORA really needed, then, was neither a stack nor a queue but a general representation of time. That's not easily accomplished, however. It's one thing to represent hours of the day—that's not too complicated—but to build into a program the sophistication required to schedule a complex series of inter-related tasks—that could take months, maybe even years. Joe had a week.

He got up and wandered out of the office. It was late in the afternoon, so he decided to catch a movie at the UC Theater, which was around the corner from his apartment, and then fix himself a bite to eat. As he walked down Hearst Avenue he kept running through the problem in his head. He had to have a queue so the retrieve-newspaper plan would come out in the right order, and yet somehow he had to get the raincoat plan at the front of it. It looked as if deciding when to put the raincoat on was as important as deciding to put it on in the first place. Hmmm. How do people know when to put on a raincoat? He paid his money and went into the theater.

He was coming out of the theater when the solution finally hit him: He would create a DoFirst plan. Everybody is familiar with the notion of doing something first: Putting on a raincoat is something you do before you go out in the rain. The whole idea of putting on a raincoat, in fact, is to put it on first. So what PAN-DORA needed, Joe decided, was a DoFirst plan that could be incorporated into the PutOn plan. That way, it could have its plan queue and still not get wet.

Joe forgot about dinner. He hurried back to Evans and logged into Kim. It took him an hour to write the code, only a few minutes to put PANDORA through its paces. This time it all went perfectly. He grinned as he switched off his terminal. All that remained was to write the paper.

The final week was a tense one. Besides Joe, three other students in the AI group were writing papers for AAAI. Yigal was writing a paper on the Context Model: a natural-language-understanding mechanism that can keep track of conversations. Peter was writing a paper about PAMELA: a story-understanding program that combines goal-based processing with a frame-based knowledge structure. Marc was writing a paper about his question-answering program, which generated better answers than earlier question-answering algorithms developed at MIT and at Yale. And Wilensky was introducing UC—the system that combines natural-language and planning abilities to come to the aid of uncertain UNIX users.

The official deadline was Thursday, but Wilensky wanted them all in hand by Wednesday. There were, of course, some complications. Yigal's program still had a couple of bugs. The rough draft of Joe's paper came in at triple the 2,000-word limit. But the person with the most serious problem was Marc. He'd just gotten a computer terminal for his home—the same blue-on-blue Zenith Data Systems terminal they used in the office. It was set up on the dining table in his living room, with a modem on a folding chair nearby so he'd be able to log into Kim through the phone lines. He wouldn't even have to dial Kim's number himself; the modem would do it automatically. Unfortunately, however, it was Passover, and as an Orthodox Jew he was forbidden to do any labor on the first and last days of the eight-day holiday, and of course on the sabbath as well. That took up a good portion of the week before the deadline.

On Monday, Yigal was still struggling with his paper. Peter was looking over Marc's paper, and Margaret was working on PHRAN, trying to get it to accept ill-formed input. The idea she was pursuing was simple: Humans can understand sentences that aren't structured correctly or that are missing a word or two; PHRAN ought to be able to do the same thing. So Margaret was trying to get it to understand the sentence "John ate apple." She'd type in "John ate apple," and PHRAN, if it understood, would respond with its internal meaning representation of the same sentence. She'd been working on this for several days now.

The only sound in the room was the dull *clack-clack, clack-clack* of the keys as the students all tried to beat their deadline.

Suddenly Margaret let out a shriek. "Oh, my God!" she cried. "Yigal! It *worked! John ate the apple.*"

Yigal went over to discuss it with her. Nobody else looked up.

On Tuesday morning, Marc got his paper back from Wilensky. The writing was good, Wilensky said, but it needed some restructuring. Marc took him a rewrite at 2:00. Peter wandered in at 5:30, having been up for the preceding thirty hours. He looked normal, if a little rumpled—baggy shorts, old T-shirt, hair sticking out in different directions. He wandered around the office for a while, then logged into Kim and started reading his paper. Marc came in from Wilensky's office with his paper in his hand. It was covered with green ink.

"What'd he say?" Peter asked.

"He said I have to make some changes."

On Wednesday, Joe decided to come in early. When he arrived, at 3:00 in the morning, everybody else had gone home. He brought some fruit salad and some cookies and tea, but he was too nervous to eat. Peter and Yigal came in around 10:00. Marc was home, unable to work until sundown Thursday.

Joe took his first draft to Wilensky shortly after lunchtime. He kept working on it until 3:00 in the afternoon, then sent it off to the printer. When Wilensky came back at 4:30, Joe's was the first one he saw. He read it, and then the others, and then he called Joe into his office. Joe came out with a grin on his face.

"He said of all the papers, it was the best one," Joe told me. "And he said he hoped our programs really did what we said they did—or at least would in the next day or two. And the other good thing was that he said I was ready to start writing my thesis."

Like PANDORA, Joe had successfully completed a simple loop —one sequence of instructions in the code of human existence. A bigger, more complicated loop awaited him. First, though, he had to do his income taxes. That was his plan for tonight.

13

Application of the AAMGAP Metatheme

Not quite two months later, Wilensky and the members of his AI team were gathered in Room 452 to hear what PANDORA could do. Paul Jacobs was absent, but everybody else was there: Marc, Peter, Yigal, and Margaret, plus two new students, Jim Martin and Jim Mayfield, who'd just joined the group. Dave Chin slipped in late and took a seat by the door. They were seated around a beige, Formica-topped table that filled the room. Blackboards surrounded them on three sides; the fourth wall was blank.

A windowless space, cold and clinical, 452 was their regular seminar room. The cold was literal, for 452 was right next door to the machine room, where the cooling requirements of Kim No-VAX and the smaller VAXes dictated a temperature that was considerably below the human comfort level. The only sound was the dull and constant roar of the machines—white noise that became a rumble in the back of your head. It lent a subtle urgency to the proceedings.

Joe arrived breathless from the Xerox room, closing the door behind him. Today he was wearing brown polyester slacks and a yellow shirt with wide brown stripes. He seemed very animated. He passed out Xeroxed copies of PANDORA's knowledge structure—her memory, so to speak. Then he drew a straight line down the middle of the blackboard. On one side of the line he wrote "Passive Automatic Processes," and on the other side he wrote "Active Controlled Processes." The room felt hermetically sealed.

It was the weekly AI seminar, and this week's topic was PANDORA. It was late spring now, some months since Yigal had given his presentation on MOPs in the fifth-floor lounge. In the time that had elapsed, Yigal had gotten his Context Model to figure out what words like *it* mean; Dave had fed PHRAN enough UNIX jargon to enable it to function as part of UC; Paul had given PHRED a Spanish-language knowledge base so it could generate sentences in Spanish as well as in English; Joe and Peter had succeeded in constructing the rudiments of their frame-based memory system for PAMELA and PANDORA; and Joe had finally managed to get PANDORA to put on her raincoat. Not only that, but a couple of weeks ago he'd taught her to deal with an umbrella as well. Now he cleared his throat and began to speak.

"Okay. Today I'm going to talk about PANDORA, the program I've been writing, implementing the theory of planning that we've developed here over the last couple of years. First I want to give you an overview of how PANDORA is organized." He paused to sweep a shock of coal-black hair off his forehead.

PANDORA, he explained, is organized into two halves. One half consists of processes that occur automatically—"things you might want to call 'unconscious,'" he said, "except that it's not clear that the other ones are conscious." The other half consists of processes that are under control.

PANDORA's goal as a program, he continued, is to detect the goals it ought to have and then to find plans for those goals, noticing any interesting interactions that might occur. One of PANDORA's most important processes, then, is the process of goal detection. He wrote "Goal Detection" on the left-hand side of the blackboard, under "Passive Automatic Processes."

On the other side he wrote "Plan Selection" and "Plan Execution." In between, he explained, there's an interface between the automatic processes and the controlled ones. That's the main control structure of PANDORA, the part that keeps everything running. This control structure operates on a data structure that's made up of queues—a queue for goals and a queue for plans. He wrote "Goal Q" and "Plan Q" across the line he'd drawn down the middle of the blackboard. His diagram was beginning to look like a cross between a Rube Goldberg construction and a flow chart.

"Okay," he said. "These are all the pieces of PANDORA, and the problem is to get them to all work together." He paused for a moment and took a deep breath.

PANDORA reacts to input, he explained, by making inferences and invoking frames. Then the goal detector comes in and does its work. Once a goal has been discovered, the next priority is to plan for the goal, so then the plan selector gets invoked. The plan selector looks for a plan that's labeled "normal plan for this goal." If there is one, it goes into the plan queue and the plan selector is through—except for an intermediate step, which is to simulate the plan.

When PANDORA simulates a plan, it processes the effects of the plan the same way it processes an external event, except that the effects of the plan are only expected to happen; they aren't treated as actual facts. "That's a thin line right now," Joe admitted.

"How thin is it?" Wilensky broke in. "Do you use a hypothetical data base?"

"I don't think I do yet," Joe said. He was a little fuzzy on this. "I marked them as hypothetical, but I don't think I have an actual separate data base. Actual facts ought to be going to a different place; I just haven't rigged up a mechanism so it knows which place to put them. It's not that complicated, but—"

"Okay," Wilensky said crisply. "Let's pursue that off-line."

"Okay. So the normal history of an event in PANDORA is: Something happens; goals get invoked; they get planned for; and if it's a normal plan, they get executed. If everything goes fine, that's what happens. The goal with PANDORA, though, is to handle situations where that path doesn't work, where something goes wrong. Let's look and see where things can go wrong."

The first place they could go wrong, Joe explained, is during plan simulation. If something does go wrong there, it's likely to lead to a goal conflict, and that will need to be dealt with before PANDORA can continue. PANDORA will then have the goal of resolving the goal conflict, which it will do by checking to see if there's a normal plan for resolving it. But there's also the possibility that goal conflict might occur during plan execution, or as the plan is being inserted into the plan queue. If that happens, it's likely to be a matter of scheduling—because at this point, conflicts might arise that are based only on time.

"What do you mean by 'time'?" Marc asked. "One thing having to happen before another?"

"One thing having to happen before another, or two things having to happen at the same time." Joe paused and swept his forehead again. "Let's see. What else isn't clear?"

Wilensky gazed distastefully at the Xeroxed sheets in front of him. "Well, first of all," he said, "maybe you could tell us what all this output is—or whatever it is. Which is it, input or output?"

"This is input," Joe said a little nervously. "This is all input. Essentially what we have here is all the knowledge for the two situations that PANDORA is currently working on—i.e., the rain situation and the running-out-of-disk-space-while-editing thing."

"What I would like," Marc said, "is if you could actually show us what goes into the rain example."

"Okay, that's probably a good idea. If we look at it in terms of this path"—Joe gestured toward the Rube Goldberg flow chart on the blackboard behind him—"upon hearing that it's morning, the Morning frame gets invoked, and that causes the goal of knowing about the world to get added to the future goals. Then the fact that it's raining happens, the Rain frame gets invoked, and that causes the rule that says if someone goes outside and they're not wearing rain gear they're going to get wet to also be added to the data base.

"At this time there aren't any more inputs, so we check for the next goal to be planned for. The only goal we have is to know what's going on in the world, so that becomes current. We look for the normal plan for that—that's at the second half of page two." He turned to the second page of the knowledge base. "What this says is, the normal plan for that is to do the following four things in sequence: Go outside, pick up the newspaper, go back inside, and read the newspaper.

"So the normal plan is chosen, and we now simulate each of the steps in the plan. We simulate going outside, and an effect of that is that we will be outside. This gets asserted into the data base, which causes us to infer that if we do that, we're gonna get wet. The fact that we're gonna get wet invokes the resolve-goal-conflict goal via the rule on page two.

"So at this point, we have the goal of resolving this goal conflict. We again go through this process of finding normal plan. Normal plan for that is to—let's see, where is that?" Joe shuffled through the knowledge base for a moment. "Okay. Here at the bottom of page two, it says the normal plan for resolving goal conflict between going outside and wanting to stay dry is to put on a raincoat —actually, to *first* put on a raincoat. So the effect of do-first is to put this at the front of the queue, whereas normally new plans get put at the end."

There were more questions. Joe answered them. At the end, he glowed with a momentary flush of pride. He had successfully MTransed to his fellow humans the workings of PANDORA—a computer program that, as near as he could tell, duplicated the planning and goal-detection algorithms of the human mind, at least as far as putting on a raincoat was concerned. The next test would be AAAI.

At the following week's seminar, Wilensky began with a little pep talk on the AAAI Conference. The letters had come in the week before: His own paper had been been accepted, as had Joe's. Everybody else had gotten rejection letters except Marc. His, it was assumed, had been lost in the mail.

The first order of business was the summer that lay before them. He himself was going to Europe.

"A lot of things," he said. "The first thing is, I'm going to be in Rome—you don't have to take notes on my itinerary, there's not going to be a quiz on this. I'm going to be traveling around Italy, and I'll leave with my secretary my address in Rome so you can get in touch with me if some emergency comes up. It *will* be an emergency if I hear from any one of you, right?" He gave them all a searching look. "But if an emergency comes up, I will be reachable.

"Now, the most important thing that will be going on this summer are the conferences in August. These are Cognitive Science, which is at the University of Michigan, and AAAI, which is at Carnegie. How many people are going to Cognitive Science?" A couple of hands went up. "How many people are going to AAAI?" Almost everybody raised a hand.

"That's about right," Wilensky said. "If you can go to Cognitive Science, that's nice, but it's really important that you go to AAAI.

"Let me explain why these conferences are important. The people whom you will meet at these conferences are your real peer group. They are people who will make important decisions about you in your life for years and years to come. I don't want to make you nervous, okay? *But*—what happens is, you'll go up to someone who's important in the field and you'll ask him a question and he'll be impressed by you. And a few years later, when your technical report or your thesis passes across this person's desk, he'll look at it. And otherwise he won't, because, remember, this person gets nine hundred technical reports and he throws most of them in a drawer.

"I cannot stress to you the importance of meeting these people and getting to know them in some sort of personal way. And it's not just the big people you should impress. You'll be meeting other graduate students, and these other graduate students, some of you may be surprised to find out, actually go on to become professors. They become your colleagues at some point, and they're going to be making all sorts of judgments about you. You'll send a grant proposal off to NSF. You're going to send papers off to conferences. And they'll say, 'Oh, that guy. I sort of didn't like that general line of work, but he seemed okay.'

"Some of you will be presenting papers at these meetings, and the same thing applies there, but all that much more so. You're going to get up and give a presentation, and people either will remember you or they won't. If you give a memorable presentation, that's important. In fact, some people say that it's better even to make a fool of yourself at one of these meetings than to go unnoticed. I'm not saying I endorse that, but—you're better off leaving some impression than no impression. It's all part of the process of becoming a person in this business."

The AAAI loop was really just a small one—nothing more than a subroutine, actually. The loop they would complete with their Ph.D. theses was larger, but even that was only a part of the big one—the one that ended with becoming a person in the business of AI. That, after all, was the goal. Wilensky had strong goals. He wanted his students to have them, too.

Of course, these were personal goals rather than societal goals. Like most of us, Wilensky and his students, while not unaware of whatever impact they might have upon the world, were more concerned with what affects them personally. But while the career path they were taking as individuals might be considered a closed loop—its steps routine and predictable, barring unforeseen circumstances—the path we are on collectively is altogether open-ended. As a species, we are standing in an open loop, heading into a future nobody knows. And we have no programmer in sight.

There are some who see AI as humans in the act of inventing their successors. There are many who see it as an act of sheer folly, like tilting at windmills. There are others who regard it as simply dangerous. These are usually fuzzy-minded humanities types, but occasionally they include people with impeccable scientific credentials. Joseph Weizenbaum, the disaffected professor who was so dismayed by the response to his ELIZA program, railed in his book against the "megalomaniac vision" of the technologist who believes that all of life can be explained in computational terms. In the hands of such people, he wrote, science—like an addictive drug—"has been converted into a slow-acting poison."

You do have to wonder about the addictive properties of science when you read a book like *The Enchanted Loom,* in which NASA cosmologist Robert Jastrow foresees the day when brain scientists will be able to dump the contents of the mind directly into the circuitry of an electronic computer. Released at last from the constraints of the flesh, this once-human mind would become the basis of a "hybrid intelligence" of man and machine. Thus through science a new race would emerge, indestructible, immortal, and free to roam the galaxies at will.

Even more timid speculations have a hallucinatory air about them. In *The Micro Millenium,* the late British computer scientist Christopher Evans speculates that the computer might put an end to war and form the basis of new religions. Some of these religions, mystical and antitechnological, might cast it in the role of Satan. "But there also remains the real chance that computers will be seen as deities," he writes, "and if they evolve into Ultra-Intelligent Machines, there may even be an element of truth in the belief."

189

The concept of the Ultra-Intelligent Machine, Evans points out, was born with the computer itself. The British computer pioneers at Bletchley—Alan Turing, the mathematician Jack Good, and others—were awestruck by the potential of their invention. It was Jack Good, an eccentric of rare form (he once nominated himself for a peerage on the grounds that it would provoke people to cry, "Good Lord, here comes Lord Good!"), who first described the concept of the Ultra-Intelligent Machine. The UIM, as Good called it, would be a computer capable of performing any intellectual feat that could be performed by a human, and performing it better.

What lies behind the concept of the UIM is the notion, widely accepted in artificial intelligence, that a computer will never be just as smart as a human being. It will be far less intelligent for many more years—a dozen, several hundred, no one really knows—and then, when all the parts are in place, it will begin to progress at an exponential rate. If that happens, we will find ourselves dealing with something like the HAL of *2001*—a ubiquitous intelligence, all-seeing and all-knowing, but so familiar that, as Keir Dullea remarked in the movie, "you begin to think of him as just another person."

Countering this vision is the belief, commonly held even by other computer scientists, that the computer can do only what it is programmed to do. In "Computing Machinery and Intelligence," the second of his two classic papers, Alan Turing calls this "Lady Lovelace's Objection"—for in her "Observations on Mr. Babbage's Analytical Engine," Byron's daughter had written reassuringly, "The Analytical Engine has no pretensions whatever to *originate* anything. It can do *whatever we know how to order it* to perform."

Turing's paper was published in 1950, six years before the Dartmouth Conference at which artificial intelligence was born. This was the paper in which he proposed the "imitation game"—what has come to be known as the "Turing test"—for deciding if a machine can think. After predicting that a machine would be capable of winning the game by the end of the century, he considered a number of "contrary views," objections that he classified as "The Theological Objection," "The Heads in the Sand Objection," "The Argument from Informality of Behavior," and so forth. Curiously, the only objection that really bothered him was the one he called "The Argument from Extrasensory Perception"—the idea that a computer will never pass as a human because it won't be telepathic.

In considering Lady Lovelace's objection, Turing suggested that she couldn't have had all the evidence, the Analytical Engine being as yet unbuilt. He also noted that she was under no obligation to claim that the machine could act on its own, even if she suspected it might. In any event, her apparent belief in the limitations of Babbage's model shouldn't be taken as evidence that all machines will remain forever unable to think for themselves. Programs already exist that enable computers to do this to a limited degree.

Many such programs work on the principle of heuristics. The heuristic approach to problem-solving, developed in the 1940s by the mathematician George Polya, is a way of proceeding by hunch: Faced with a vast array of possibilities, one follows general rules of thumb to arrive at a solution. Heuristic programming techniques have been particularly useful in domains such as chess, where the number of possible moves and countermoves is too vast even for a computer to consider. By exploring only the moves that appear most promising, chess-playing programs cut the number of board positions they have to consider from several billion to something like 20 or 30 million. This makes them unpredictable enough to beat humans, including the humans who write them—which, as one AI researcher noted in *Scientific American*, does make Lady Lovelace's objection seem rather misleading.

But chess-playing programs are so old hat these days, they barely qualify as artificial intelligence anymore. The interesting programs that use heuristics now combine them with enough world knowledge to produce practical results. One heuristically based program, EURISKO, actually learns new heuristics on its own. Developed by Douglas Lenat, a Stanford professor who's associated with Xerox PARC, EURISKO can deal with anything from mathematical puzzles to intergalactic warfare. One of its greatest triumphs, reported in an article in *Fortune*, came in the championship rounds of a computer game in which contestants design their own star fleets and then pit them against each other in battle. EURISKO won by analyzing the rules and coming up with a highly counterintuitive but logically unassailable principle of ship design. Its next task was to design micro-chips—VLSI circuits so complicated that the human mind can barely comprehend them.

By comparison, PANDORA seemed rather limited: All it could do was put on a raincoat, and it didn't need heuristics to do that. It had been programmed to detect the goals it should have, to detect conflicts between those goals, and to find plans for dealing with them. The plans themselves were canned—go outside and pick up the newspaper, put on a raincoat, and so forth. Humans have plans that are canned in exactly the same way: The put-on-a-raincoat plan, for example, is programmed into us at an early age by our mothers, who become very exasperated when we fail to apply it. But humans also have the ability to invent new plans, to apply old plans to unforeseen circumstances, to innovate. PAN-DORA didn't. "That's somebody else's thesis," Joe declared.

Before he wrote his own thesis, though, Joe would have to get PANDORA to handle more complicated situations. He'd have to put it in predicaments where it would have to plan and replan until it found a plan that worked. He'd have to get it to do a lot of new examples. Eventually he'd end up getting it to invoke the Earthquake frame and stand under a doorway if it felt the floor shaking—but not if it looked down the hall and saw a forklift coming in with a new computer. He'd get it to solve his old problem of how to watch the Monday night football game when it learns its mother is in the hospital after an emergency appendectomy. In fact, he'd even end up rebuilding its memory so it could come up with a novel plan—so it could actually do something innovative. He'd fix it so it could decide to hop on a roller coaster if someone were chasing it through an amusement park.

But all this was off in the future; for AAAI, the raincoat would be enough. After all, nobody else had built a computer program that knew when to put on a raincoat. And to the best of his knowledge, nobody else had built a computer program that could generate its own goals, either. A program with its own goals brought you one step closer to a computer with an independent mind. If machines were ever to function as sentient beings—as space explorers, for example, probing distant galaxies—one thing they'd need would be goals of their own. That's why AI researchers at NASA's Jet Propulsion Laboratory were working on the same problems.

There was one sense in which Lady Lovelace's objection would hold anyway, for PANDORA and every other program under development. Computers might be programmed in a way that would enable them to do something not specifically included in their instructions; they were not necessarily the programmer's slave. But there was as yet no way to program them to do things that were wholly outside their realm of expertise. There was no medical-diagnosis program, for example, that would develop an interest in medieval literature if you left it running long enough. For that matter, there was no medical-diagnosis program that would develop an interest even in medical literature. In that sense, still, a computer could do only what it was programmed to do.

Given the uses to which AI programs may be put, this has significant consequences. Some eighteen months after PAN-DORA put on its raincoat, ARPA outlined a response to the Japanese fifth-generation computer effort. By spending $600 million in five years, ARPA hopes to spur advances in artificial intelligence, computer architecture, and microelectronics which will combine to produce weapons of "unprecedented capabilities." Among these are a personalized "pilot's associate" for fighter jocks, and land-roving robots for reconnaissance and attack. "This is a very sexy area to the military," a high-ranking ARPA official told *Newsweek*, "because you can imagine all kinds of neat, interesting things you could send off on their own little missions around the world."

Also planned for development is a complex battle management system (BMS) capable of forecasting enemy actions, generating possible responses, evaluating the various options, implementing the one the commander chooses, and reporting on the results. Initially this system would be used by a naval carrier battle group (testing is to be conducted on the U.S.S. *Carl Vinson*), but eventually, the report notes, it could be applied in other areas, including missile defense. As outlined by ARPA, the BMS sounds much like HAL of *2001*: a distributed intelligence with speaking and listening abilities and virtual control of the ship. A space-based version would depend on radiation-hardened gallium-arsenide chips instead of silicon and would likely be a key component of President Reagan's projected "Star Wars" defense. As such it would have effective control of the nuclear arsenal.

The report observes that "commanders remain particularly concerned about the role autonomous systems would play during the transition from peace to hostilities, when rules of engagement may be altered quickly. An extremely stressing example of such a case is the projected defense against strategic nuclear missiles, where systems must react so quickly that it is likely that almost complete reliance will have to be placed on automated systems."

Their concern would seem justified. If intelligent computers are employed as strategic "management systems," just how intelligent will they be? John McCarthy of Stanford has pointed out that computerized consultants such as MYCIN, the expert system that diagnoses bacterial infections in the blood, have no real idea of what they're doing. MYCIN contains a lot of facts about bacteria and blood, but it has no knowledge of doctors or hospitals, of life or death, or even of the patient. All it does is follow a series of "pattern/action rules" that instruct it to identify certain patterns and to suggest certain actions to be performed—if this, then do that; if that, then do the other thing. Being restricted in this way is what enables it to work, because that keeps the number of facts it has to know at a manageable level. But it doesn't enable it to respond to the unexpected, or to have any understanding of its role in human affairs.

The Pentagon hopes to have its intelligent computer systems in operation during the next decade. Will these systems know anything about the effects of nuclear war, or will they function according to the dictates of simple if/then rules? Will they even know what humans are, and what this planet means to us? Who will do their programming? The answer is crucial, because in the larger sense, what we get out will be what we put in.

Does it make sense, I asked Wilensky, to program computers with common sense?

He replied with a snort. "If you want them to have common sense it does."

So choices have to be made, and opportunities present themselves. Maybe computers will be an improvement. Humans, as Wilensky pointed out, are not well-engineered for the society they've developed. Not long after he made that remark, the president of the Carnegie Corporation gave a lecture in which he lamented a fundamental "bug" in human nature. In humans, it seems, the need for close attachment and the capacity for aggression are closely linked. "The human tendency to react with fear and hostility to strangers has roots in our prehuman past," he declared. "We justify our slaughter of outside groups by our need to protect our own."

He could have been talking about Lebanon, or Central America, or World War III. Throughout millions of years of evolutionary development, the instinct to gather together in small, belligerent, tightly bonded packs was demonstrably sound. In the twentieth century it suddenly became extremely maladaptive. Technology has outpaced evolution. The brain of the ancestral mammal—the small, furry, rat-like creature that sees provocation in the face of a stranger—that brain now controls the fate of the earth.

With fifth-generation technology, it's not impossible to envision a future in which our robots fight their robots somewhere out in space and humans cheer them on from the sidelines. Maybe the entire conflict could be run in simulation mode with advanced computer-graphics displays for the benefit of civilian and military commanders who crave *Star Wars* excitement. Or perhaps computers, lacking the evolutionary flaws of the human brain and programmed with the Preserve-Endangered-State goal, could decide to end the arms race unilaterally. Unfortunately, however, none of this is really very likely. After all, if humans aren't well engineered for the society they've developed, will the machines they build be any better designed? Is there any guaranty that intelligent machines will even act in our interest?

Wilensky was astonished at my naïveté. "Most of the machines we've created so far haven't acted in our interest," he declared. "Why should these? Of course not! It's not even likely. Whether or not they act in their own interest is another matter. But of course they're gonna be abused by somebody, as every other thing humans have ever done was, starting with fire. The precedent is not good."

It was the last week of spring quarter. Tuesday. The sky was radiant with sunlight. The window of the AI office brought in splashes of color: bright blue sky, deep green hills, red tile roof, soft gray concrete. Joe was at his terminal as usual, logged into Kim.

The ARPA man had been on campus the day before. He was an army major attached to IPTO, the agency's Information Processing Technologies Office, and he'd flown out from Washington for the day to interview faculty members in the computer science division. It was their annual checkup: Every spring, ARPA sent somebody out to see what these people were doing with their new computers and their research contracts. The interviews were conducted in a brisk and military fashion. Each professor got fifteen minutes to explain his work.

Joe was a little uncomfortable about all this. He was glad it was Wilensky and not he who had to talk to the ARPA man. Joe was the kind of person who subscribed to *Mother Jones* and *The Progressive*. Money from the military was something he'd just as soon not think about. But if you lived in America and you wanted to model the mind on a digital computer, you had to let the Pentagon pay for it. Everybody knew that. It was part of the deal.

Joe had just come back from the post office. It had been exactly two months since his original AAAI deadline, and today the final draft had to be sent in. He'd made a few small changes, like adding a one-paragraph abstract at the beginning to sum up. The language was suitably dry and academic: ". . . detects its own goals in an event-driven fashion, dynamically interleaving the creation, execution, and revision of its plans." He'd mailed in a new draft of Marc's paper as well—for to everyone's surprise, including Marc's, his paper had been accepted. The letter had been lost in the mail, but it was an acceptance notice, not a rejection slip.

Joe pulled out an extra copy of Marc's paper and started reading. He got halfway down the first page and then sat up with a start. *"FAUSTUS?"* he cried, turning to Marc aghast. "What is *FAUSTUS?"*

At the beginning of the fourth paragraph, where "PAMELA" had appeared before, Marc's paper now made reference to "FAUSTUS."

Marc shrugged. "Peter's calling his program FAUSTUS."

"FAUSTUS?" Joe was flabbergasted. "He's calling it FAUSTUS? Why didn't he tell me? I called it PAMELA!"

Marc shrugged. "I dunno."

A technopop band called the Human League was on the radio. They had a Top Forty hit with a lockstep sound: "These are the things/These are the things/The things that dreams are made of." Joe decided to query Peter by electronic mail. Like Marc, Peter had gotten a remote terminal and was spending most of his time at home. Joe typed furiously at his little desk:

```
9> mail norvig
Subject: FAUSTUS?!?!?!
What does it stand for? Why didn't you tell me? I
referred to it as PAMELA in my paper. And now
it's too late to fix.
```

When he got no response, Joe went to Kim's directory, which listed all the files stored on the machine. There, along with PAN-DORA.L and PHRAN.L and PHRED.L and so forth, he found a file called FAUSTUS.L—the *.L* indicating it was written in LISP. There was no file marked PAMELA.L. Joe was incredulous. "You mean there's a file called FAUSTUS?" He typed in a command and pulled it onscreen.

"'FAUSTUS,' he said, reading from the screen. "Frame-Activated Unified Story-Understanding System." He exhaled slowly. "That's a good name," he said at last. "Frame . . . story-understanding . . . unified, which means there's all sorts of other stuff in there . . . hmmm . . ."

A list of alternatives appeared onscreen as well—other names Peter had evidently been considering but had decided against. There was STU—"STory-Understander." STUMP—"STory-Understanding and Memory Program." FRUSTRUM—"FRame-based Unified Story-Understanding Model." Clearly FAUSTUS was the best choice. Even Joe thought so.

"Hmmm," he mused, pulling at his beard. "Except for UC, that's our first program without a *p* in front of it. Only last weekend, that file was called PAMELA."

The next day was the last day of the quarter. The AI office was buzzing with activity. Everybody was finishing up one thing, getting ready to do something else. Margaret and the junior grad students—David, Marc, and Paul—had come to campus to take the last of their exams. David and Marc would be going to AAAI, but Paul was going to lead a group of high-school students on a white-water canoeing expedition in Quebec, near Hudson's Bay. Yigal would be presenting his paper at the Cognitive Science Conference in Ann Arbor. Right now he was logged into Kim, running a program that was automatically generating random long-division problems for his daughter, Bosmi, who wanted to practice her arithmetic.

Bartlett Mel, the undergraduate who'd spoken at the end of last quarter's "Should Robots Have Civil Rights?" seminar, popped in the door. This quarter he'd taken Wilensky's introductory AI course, along with Philosophy 101. He'd been surprised to discover the close ties between AI and philosophy. In philosophy he'd read Heidegger's *Question Concerning Technology*. Heidegger did not impress him, Dreyfus's enthusiasm notwithstanding. He pulled out a book and read aloud. "Enframing is the gathering together that belongs to that setting-upon which sets upon man and puts him in position to reveal the real, in the mode of ordering, as standing reserve," it read. In the margin he'd scrawled, "Well put!"

Paul and Marc took off to get a cup of coffee on Euclid Avenue. Joe walked in with an invitation to be listed in *Who's Who in Robotics*. "They want you to include all the other *Who's Who*'s you're listed in," he laughed. "I guess I won't waste their time trying to make PANDORA sound like a robot."

Wilensky stuck his head in the door to announce that he'd been getting calls from corporate headhunters. One of them had said he was representing a major aerospace company in Washington State. "Can you figure out who that would be?" Another was from a drug company in Los Angeles. "She was weird." But the message was clear: If you ever got tired of teaching, there would be plenty of companies ready to hire you at $100,000 and up.

Wilensky dashed off for the airport. He'd be in Rome the next morning.

Joe looked troubled. "I dunno," he said. "Do I wanna make a

hundred thousand a year?" The answer, he quickly realized, was no. His goal was to figure out how the mind works. No multinational conglomerate in its right mind was going to pay him $100,000 a year to do that.

But that was the long term. How about short-term goals? Joe ran a finger on the team. The finger was a program that looked for a file called ".project" and a file called ".plan." There was a .project file and a .plan file for everybody in the group, as well as for the group itself. The .project file was supposed to be a one-line summary of who you were and what you were doing; the .plan file was more complete. Joe's own plan file was structured like a computer program:

```
cobegin
  Process 1 begin
  1. Figure out how automatic inference and
     memory processes work.
  2. Build a program to do this and
     incorporate this into PANDORA.
  3. Figure out a representation scheme for
     the knowledge we have about how to
     do/use things and incorporate this
     into PANDORA.
  4. Represent everything there is to know
     about UNIX in this scheme and incorp . . .
     . . .
  k. Go back to 1.
  Process 1 end
  Process 2 begin
    Work on thesis.
  Process 2 end
coend
```

He'd programmed himself to complete a loop, in other words, with instructions to perform two operations in parallel—expand PANDORA and write his thesis. Other .plans were by turns fanciful or brusque. Margaret's for example, said, "To finish 152a in the near future, graduate, and stay a student forevermore, evermore . . ." Paul's, on the other hand, was much more abrupt: "I will be on vacation until the end of August," it said. "I should check in around September 5."

Perhaps the most carefully precisiated .plan, however, was Peter's. It was organized into plan, goal, and theme, and it read as follows:

```
Plan:
  Figure out reminding, then inferencing, then
  explaining, then code it.
Goal:
  Discover a coherent theory of memory structure
  and understanding.
Theme:
  AAMGAP
```

It was the AAMGAP metatheme: Achieve As Many Goals As Possible. In *Planning and Understanding: A Computational Approach to Human Reasoning*—the book he'd just finished writing—Wilensky had listed AAMGAP as one of the four metathemes he'd encountered in his theory of planning. AAMGAP was the one responsible for detecting goal conflicts. For humans, as for machines, it was a rule to live by.

Epilogue

The Skibo ballroom was jammed. Carnegie-Mellon was throwing a reception for the AAAI Conference, and some 1,200 practicing AI researchers had turned out for the event. The ballroom was a sea of name tags, most of them featuring letters of the alphabet in a variety of configurations: MIT, IBM, USC, SRI, TRW. Three-piece suits mingled with flowing gray beards; crisp green army uniforms with shoulder-length hair; drooping T-shirts with blue blazers and white turtlenecks. No one could accuse the AI community of mindless uniformity.

"Have you considered a future in Texas Instruments?"

A corporate type had buttonholed an anemic-looking young man in worn-out dungarees and sneakers. The name tag pinned to the concave chest read "Carnegie-Mellon." Obviously a professional grad student. The question drew a look of mild distaste. "Are you offering me a job?"

"Well, uh—yes."

"Where?"

"Dallas."

"Forget it."

Skibo Hall is a Fifties-modern building, plate glass and brick, about as old as artificial intelligence itself. It sits on a grassy field at the edge of the CMU campus. Carnegie-Mellon looks much like the rest of Pittsburgh: hard, gritty, no-nonsense. If Stanford has the air of a California technology ranch and MIT the feel of a Yankee engineering mill, CMU—the old Carnegie Tech—looks like the slag from some robber baron's steel fortune. Which, of course, is what it is.

Marc spied Joe and came over to greet him. "How long have you been here?" he asked.

Joe was nonplussed. The question was so imprecise. "Do you mean here two days or here five minutes?"

Roger Schank was standing nearby—a burly man, tall and bearded, with tufts of curly black hair receding from his forehead. Ferociously intelligent, he'd be a formidable personage in any environment, but nowhere more so than in the presence of the people whose field he's turned upside down in the past decade. During his years at Yale, Schank had become the *enfant terrible* of artificial intelligence, the man who showed the giants of the field what they were doing wrong. It was as an undergraduate here at Carnegie that he'd started the process.

In a sense, of course, the giants were unassailable. In the early days, when Minsky and McCarthy and Newell and Simon were all young, the task was not so much to find the answers as to find the right questions. Schank and others like him have been able to stand on their shoulders and profit from their mistakes. In the Fifties, for example, Newell and Simon of Carnegie-Mellon pursued what's known as the "cognitive simulation" approach to AI. Cognitive simulation to them meant applying theorem-proving techniques to mathematical problems and puzzles. Schank's cognitive-modeling approach also has the goal of mimicking human mental processes, but the processes he studies and the methods he employs are quite different. He's interested in the psychology of language and memory, and he doesn't think the human mind is in any way governed by the rigors of mathematical logic.

The babble of the cocktail party receded into the background as we stepped through a sliding glass door and entered the hard-edged landscape. "I've always been interested in psychology," Schank said. "I think my reputation in psychology, although I'm not a psychologist, is fairly strong, and the reason is that scripts were a new idea to psychologists—as were plans and goals and inferences and a lot of the other things I've been doing.

"At the time I started talking to them, they were all heavily influenced by Chomsky. A lot of people were getting really sick of the Chomskyan paradigm—the idea of making a formal model of language, with a bias toward the idea that syntax is central—because it just wasn't working. They were the people who subsequently glommed on to the things that I was working on. But psychologists will always say the same thing about me, which is that I've done lots of suggestive things and that they still have to do their experiments to prove it. I won't argue."

His relationship with philosophers, I remarked, seemed a little less cordial.

"I think the nature of how we answer questions is so different from how philosophers answer questions that we tend to raise their hackles," Schank replied. "But the intentions are the same. All the issues that we're interested in, intention and belief and language—those are all philosophical questions. The difference is that we have a tool, right? We have this computer. And what it does for us is it tests our theories.

"If you look at a philosopher's theories, you'll discover that they aren't algorithmic at all! That's really the difference. We have a prejudice toward theories that say 'first this step, then that step,' rather than philosophers' theories, which tend to be holistic. They step back and say, 'Well, there are these general things going on.' Computer scientists tend to get very antsy when they hear that, because they want to know what's first and what's second.

"But the computer shouldn't be taken too seriously. What we're interested in is building algorithms. What are the human algorithms? One way or another, humans have algorithms—and one way or another, I'd like to find out what they are. The physical hardware manifestation of those algorithms is obviously going to be different because computers aren't like brains, and how computers embody algorithms is not of any great interest. I don't care how they do it. Blips or blaps or lights or chemicals—who cares?"

What about Dreyfus, who's arguing that it's impossible to discover these algorithms and represent them in any formal way at all?

Schank gave me an exasperated look. "Oh, that's just because he's a mystic! I mean, look. What does he mean, 'it's not possible'? There's always somebody standing around saying it's not possible, so you do it!

"The question is, what are you trying to represent? I think Dreyfus is offended by the notion that if you represent some simple thing, you've represented the essence of it. And I think he's *right* on that subject. But one way or another, that stuff is represented in the brain, isn't it? It's represented by some discrete entity—chemicals or electrical states of neurons or whatever. And so all we're saying is that there must be some way to represent it, period. I'm saying that there's an algorithm that people go through to be able to talk. I don't know how you can argue with that! One way or another, we do it, and all I'm saying is that I'd like to find out how we do it. People who say it's mystical and *you can't know*—I don't know what kind of argument that is."

But how can you get at the algorithms beneath human thought, I asked, when humans seem to think so differently from each other?

"I don't think people think as differently as you might imagine," he said. "People have different predispositions. A person from the outside world will say, 'What are you talking about? I know Jane, and Jane thinks so differently from Joe!' Yes, of course she does, but in terms of the underlying apparatus, the basic things they're manipulating inside their heads—they're not manipulating different *things*, they're making different *choices* when they do the manipulations. My restaurant script doesn't look like your restaurant script because I've been to different restaurants, but we both have information about restaurants in them.

"What you mean by 'people think differently' is that people have different experiences which force them to different conclusions—and the machine also would have different experiences. I think that ultimately, when we talk about all-knowing machines, they'll probably be quite different from people because their experience will be so incredibly different. They won't have had the experience of eating or sleeping or making love or being born or any of those things. And they will have had the experience of sitting in the same place all the time and having people ask them the same questions over and over—which might make them very adept at answering those questions."

All-knowing machines? Will such things ever exist?

"It's hard to say what will *ever* exist, but in the near future, if we are successful, one would imagine that you would find little specialist machines that would be out in the world. The all-knowing machines would still be in the laboratory, because there's this massive information problem of how to pay attention to one thing and not another and not screwing up. But I think there'll be an all-knowing machine someday. That's what we're about."

Doesn't it give you pause?

"No, on the contrary. Give me pause as a citizen? *Look,* you can spend your life worrying about somebody doing something bad with your stuff. I'm certain that somebody's going to do something bad with my stuff, because they do it with everything. It's always been the case. I think the likelihood of somebody doing something bad with AI is one hundred percent. But since I think that's also true of everything else, I think the problem is perhaps to change the nature of people before you worry about the tools they have. And frankly, I'm a lot less concerned with me being in charge of those tools."

But how much are you in charge of it, if the Pentagon is footing the bill?

"Well . . . they're a rather benign bill-footer. They don't really tell you what you have to do, and you don't have to wrap it up all that fast, and they often intend to be using it for purposes that aren't all that malevolent in any case. I don't know. Yeah, sure, you can say the CIA's going to use it to try to eavesdrop on everybody in the world, and they probably will, but—there's nothing I can do about that.

"There's always some kind of trade-off. Every time we provide one good thing, we provide the possibility to do another bad thing. You can make bombers, and you can make people be able to see the whole world. Telephones—we all talk to each other, and people eavesdrop on the conversation. And I don't know that we aren't supposed to make telephones or airplanes or anything else. My hope is that we can make them, and that we can learn to have a sensible society." He retreated into his head for a moment, then looked off into the trees. "I don't *believe* that, but I hope it."

On the second evening of the AAAI Conference, there was a dinner/dance on a pair of riverboats as they made their way up and down the Ohio and the Monongahela. Schank and Wilensky were absent, because every year at AAAI or IJCAI, its international counterpart, Schank hosts a reunion banquet for all his former students from Yale. But Joe went along, as did his friend Mike Deering, the former schoolmate who went on to do research in computer vision for Fairchild in San Jose.

The riverboats were standard tourist barges that had been enthusiastically gussied up in an attempt to evoke the paddle-wheel steamers of yore. They had red flounce curtains on the windows and red anchor appliqués on the walls and white wrought-iron railings around the decks and Krazy Kong machines in the corners. Hanging off their sterns were little imitation paddle wheels that spun helplessly in the water. It was a Disneyland tour of Pittsburgh: There were the ancient steel mills, abandoned and collapsing now; there were the gleaming downtown office towers, testament to the city's booming new service economy; overhead was a flotilla of bridges, humming with traffic and strung with lights.

"I have a theorem about vision," Deering cried as he emerged from the night.

"A theorem about vision?" inquired Joe.

"Yes. It's harder to find people in the dark."

"And you won't find anyone from Yale here at all."

"That's too bad," Mike said. "I wanted to at least try to talk to Schank."

"Apparently Schank didn't like the menu."

"Schank doesn't like to talk to people," Mike retorted. "At the first Cognitive Science Conference, we were all steaming about the fact that we had something to talk to him about and he wouldn't do it. He was in what he called 'social mode,' which meant he wouldn't talk about AI."

Joe chuckled. He was in social mode himself. This was, after all, his third conference in a month. After the Cognitive Science

Conference in Ann Arbor, he'd flown to Pittsburgh and rented a car so he could drive to New England—through upstate New York, Vermont, and New Hampshire to Maine, then down the coast to Boston. He'd stayed for a few days in Newton with Dave Chin and his family, who'd taken him into town for his first taste of Legal Seafood.

Legal Seafood is a popular Boston restaurant that's regarded by Schankians as a landmark of artificial intelligence. It violates the restaurant script. It's one of the few nice restaurants in America —maybe the only one—where you pay your check before you eat your meal. Schank refers to it frequently in his talks. "I took a copy of the placemat," Joe said, "which explains why they do that. It essentially says they don't want to hold you up when you're waiting for the tab. I'm sure it means they don't want you to sit there any longer than you have to."

From Boston, Joe had driven back to Pittsburgh for a LISP conference that preceded AAAI. Then he'd started thinking about the talk he had to give on PANDORA. He decided he wanted to make some mention of the myth of Pandora in his talk. The myth was something he dimly remembered from ninth grade—how curiosity had gotten the best of Pandora and led her to open this magic box, only to have all the evils of the world fly out; and how then in despair she'd looked inside and found hope still resting on the bottom. He'd looked for a connection between the myth and the program when he'd chosen the name, but he hadn't been able to find one.

It was late in the evening now, and the riverboats were returning to their slips. A middle-aged man had pulled out a guitar and was leading a singalong on deck. A circle of people took shape around him. They joined in, their voices ragged and off-key and laden with nostalgia, as he strummed the chords to "Michael, Row the Boat Ashore" and "Where Have All the Flowers Gone?" For a moment it could have been a campfire surrounded by teenagers in the middle Sixties. But this was no scout camp in the woods. It was a tour boat on the Monongahela River in the summer of 1982, and the people singing the folk songs were grownups now, grown-ups whose curiosity had led them to tinker with that mysterious box we call the computer.

If there were indeed a connection between Pandora the myth and PANDORA the program, curiosity would be the key. What are the workings of the human mind? How can they be modeled on a digital computer? Those were the questions, and to answer one you would have to answer the other. It was fun, it was a game, it was serious business. And of course there was the possibility that in opening up these questions, certain unpredictable forces would be unleashed. That was always a risk of science.

Joe's talk was scheduled for 2:30 on Friday afternoon. It was one of the last of the conference, coming after such presentations as "Tracking Known Three-Dimensional Objects" (by a scientist from the Jet Propulsion Laboratory), "Distributed Bayesian Processing for Belief Maintenance in Hierarchical Inference Systems" (from UCLA), "SWIRL: An Object-Oriented Air Battle Simulator" (the Rand Corporation), and "A Program That Learns to Solve Rubik's Cube" (Carnegie-Mellon). Like all the others, he had twenty minutes.

At 2:35—the conference was running late, but not by much—he walked onstage at Lawrence Hall, a mammoth auditorium at the University of Pittsburgh, just across Panther Hollow from Carnegie-Mellon. With huge cylinders and portholes and parts of spheres protruding from its walls and ceiling, the auditorium had the futuristic appearance of a space galleon. Also, like the brain, it was split down the middle into two halves. Joe had the right half, with several hundred people in attendance.

His talk was basically his paper: a spirited, though technical, description of the workings of PANDORA. He described the overall control loop that told PANDORA what to do: If there's an event, process it; if there's a goal, plan for it; if there are plans, execute them. He explained the three queues—one each for events, goals, and plans—and the difference between the automatic processes (memory, inference, goal detection) and the control processes (plan selection, plan simulation, plan execution). He described PANDORA's decision to put on the raincoat, and he explained that although the pieces of PANDORA are very simple, the power of PANDORA lies in the way they are put together.

And at the end he brought in the myth—except that instead of envy and spite and revenge, what this PANDORA had to offer was something else, something more in tune with the AI point of view. "We opened PANDORA's box," he declared, smiling broadly as he slipped a diagram into the slide projector in front of him, "and all these things came popping out. Memory, inference, and noticing happen automatically and are shared by a story-understanding program. Goal detection is in fact one of the most important parts of PANDORA. And then we have the control processes, selection, projection, and execution, which are organized so that they can be interrupted by new goals and thus work flexibly. And if you're confused about how all this works, in the bottom of the box, just as in the myth of Pandora, we have hope—which is the thesis that I'm working on. Thank you."

There was enthusiastic applause, and Joe walked off the stage to be besieged by the more curiosity-driven of his peers.